MAKING
ARTISAN BREADS
IN THE BREAD MACHINE

MAKING
ARTISAN BREADS
IN THE BREAD MACHINE

Beautiful Loaves and Flatbreads from All Over the World

MICHELLE ANDERSON

HARVARD
COMMON
PRESS

Brimming with creative inspiration, how-to projects, and useful information to enrich your everyday life, Quarto Knows is a favorite destination for those pursuing their interests and passions. Visit our site and dig deeper with our books into your area of interest: Quarto Creates, Quarto Cooks, Quarto Homes, Quarto Lives, Quarto Drives, Quarto Explores, Quarto Gifts, or Quarto Kids.

© 2021 Quarto Publishing Group USA Inc.

First Published in 2021 by The Harvard Common Press, an imprint of The Quarto Group,
100 Cummings Center, Suite 265-D,
Beverly, MA 01915, USA.
T (978) 282-9590 F (978) 283-2742 QuartoKnows.com

The Harvard Common Press titles are also available at discount for retail, wholesale, promotional, and bulk purchase. For details, contact the Special Sales Manager by email at specialsales@quarto.com or by mail at The Quarto Group, Attn: Special Sales Manager, 100 Cummings Center, Suite 265-D, Beverly, MA 01915, USA.

25 24 23 22 21   2 3 4 5

ISBN: 978-1-59233-992-1

Digital edition published in 2021
eISBN: 978-1-63159-980-4

Library of Congress Cataloging-in-Publication Data
Anderson, Michelle, author.
Making artisan breads in the bread machine : beautiful and delectable loaves and flatbreads from all over the world / Michelle Anderson.
ISBN 9781592339921 (trade paperback) | ISBN 9781631599804 (ebook)
1. Automatic bread machines. 2. Bread. 3. Cooking (Bread). 4. Cookbooks.
LCC TX769 .A6645 2020 (print) | LCC TX769 (ebook) | DDC 641.8⅕—dc23
LCCN 2020025394 (print) | LCCN 2020025395 (ebook)

Design: Debbie Berne
Cover Images: Alison Bickel Photography; Except for top right Shutterstock
Photography: Alison Bickel Photography; Except for pages 25, 28-34 Shutterstock

Printed in China

As always, to my mother, Thea, who never baked a loaf of bread in her life, but who would have sat with a glass of wine keeping me company, making me laugh. I miss you every minute of every day.

Contents

- - - - - - - - - - - -

Preface

My very first real chef job in the early 1990s was in a charming little restaurant located in an old farmhouse on a rural highway in Ontario, Canada. I was the "morning and lunch chef," and my job included baking all the bread, rolls, and desserts for service. This meant arriving at 4 a.m. five days a week and working solo until the rest of the staff meandered in at 9:30 a.m. We had no fancy mixer with a dough hook or proofing drawers. I was lucky when the oven didn't blow my eyebrows off when I manually lit the gas each morning. I required all that extra time because I kneaded all the dough by hand—and that takes a long time.

So, I gathered my ingredients, put a suitably rocking '80s song on the boom box, and got to work. I can tell you that kneading bread dough is hard work—and excellent therapy if your life isn't going well. You push and pummel, using every muscle in your shoulders, arms, forearms, and fingers to get the perfect texture. There is a satisfying moment when the dough seems to come alive under your hands, suddenly elastic and almost silky. When you stretch it between your fingers, it is translucent. This is called the windowpane test, although at the time I didn't know it had a name. After kneading, I set bowls and bowls of covered dough all around my drafty kitchen to rise, each batch finishing at a different time. The smell of active yeast permeated my hair and clothes for the rest of the day.

At around 9 a.m., my bread baking was complete and the golden stacked loaves and piles of buns formed into pretty knots adorned the kitchen. Rarely in my life have I experienced the quiet pride and sense of accomplishment all that perfectly baked fragrant bread produced. That feeling of satisfaction is what this book is about. I want you to create beautiful loaves of bread that delight you, but without all the backbreaking work. You might already be a veteran bread baker or maybe are new to this world of yeast and flour. No matter your experience level, you will find a wealth of information and tempting recipes in these chapters.

PART I

BREAD DEMYSTIFIED

Getting Started

What Is Artisan Bread?

Let's consider the term "artisan bread." There is no real definition or regulation in a culinary sense of what "artisan" means, just a vague idea of what people think it should mean. For some, the term signifies strict ingredients and procedures. Serious artisan bread bakers might use only four ingredients—flour, water, salt, and yeast— and not ordinary yeast or flour, only wild yeast (page 27) and hand-milled flours. Then, the bread is baked in a handmade oven or specialty oven of some sort to mimic ancient techniques. The commitment to this version of "artisan" is commendable and the bread produced is unique, but for most home bakers, this process is not feasible. So, artisan bread in the scope of this book encompasses traditional bread made with quality ingredients, no preservatives, and with care—a broader scope than the four-ingredient template used by some purists. All recipes are baked in a bread machine or prepped in the bread machine and baked in a traditional oven. Ultimately, artisan bread in this book is defined by the skill, time, and love put into its creation.

Why Bake Your Own Bread?

Because bread is so readily available everywhere, even in little convenience stores on the corner, why take the time to make our own bread? The main reason most people make their own bread is the satisfaction and pleasure of taking a fragrant, golden loaf of bread out of the oven or bread maker knowing you created it with your own hands. There is something almost primal being part of such an incredible history, stretching back thousands of years to the first people who added water to pounded plant fibers and cooked this mixture on a hot rock by a fire. Now, bread machines are a long way from hot stones and ingredients have evolved, but that satisfaction of creation is still evident and rewarding.

Another reason to make your own bread is the control you have over the ingredients, eliminating strange chemical compounds, dyes, and preservatives. Anyone on a special diet can attest to the difficulty of finding high quality bread in a supermarket that suits your specific needs. This is also important if you or a family member has allergies and cannot have ingredients such as dairy or nuts. Making your own bread can save you money as well, probably just a dollar here and a dollar there, but that can add up over time. You pay for not only the bread but also the packaging and labor of the baker when you purchase a commercially prepared loaf.

Unless you buy specialty loaves with heaps of ingredients and no additives, homemade bread is more nutritious and better tasting than most store-bought options. There is, undoubtedly, delicious bread available from talented bakers committed to creating unique quality bread, but you will pay more for that product. Homemade bread is usually higher in protein, healthy carbs, and fiber as well as vitamins and minerals. The texture and taste of your own bread are often superior because it is handcrafted a single loaf or two at a time rather than mass-produced. This attention and care are what designate home-baked bread as artisan bread.

How to Make Artisan Bread in a Machine

As stated earlier, there is no "official" definition of the word "artisan" concerning food, and, often, the label is used more for marketing purposes than a description of the actual product. When you think of artisan bread, I will bet you conjure an image of a thickly crusted, slightly irregular loaf, maybe with a scattering of seeds or asymmetrical slashes across the top. This is certainly a good depiction—but not the only one. This lovely imagined loaf was hand processed, made with carefully chosen high quality ingredients, and created in small batches—the same way you would make bread in your own kitchen, utilizing a bread machine for the dough or whole loaf. Artisan bread bakers continuously advance their skills, tweak the recipes, and improve their techniques, as will you over the course of your breadmaking journey. A bread machine just makes it possible for you to create gorgeous artisan bread and do everything else you need to do in your life.

The simple answer to how to make artisan bread in a bread machine is to put the ingredients in, select a program, and press Start. It is that easy. The machine gives you options: Just set it and forget it, or take the perfectly formed dough from the machine and handcraft the loaf yourself. These options mean you can change your plans if something comes up, or even if the weather changes. Imagine a scorching-hot day, with or without air conditioning, and how warm your kitchen gets when you turn on a conventional oven. I know we live on salads in summer to avoid this situation. A bread machine uses less power than a standard coffee maker and will not increase the temperature in your home. In this case, you would just leave the bread in the machine rather than wrestle with overheated dough and a 400°F (200°C) oven.

Don't get caught up in anyone else's idea of artisan bread, though. If you make your bread in your home with care and love for yourself or others, it is artisan bread. Bread is a special food, a symbol of family and connection. The tradition of "breaking bread" is one of the oldest human traditions, meaning "welcome" and a celebration of similarities and differences. It honors the guest and the act is inclusive in nature. Keep this in mind when you proudly place a loaf of golden bread on your own table, whether it is a uniform rectangle out of a bread machine or a slightly more rustic baguette from the oven.

The Recipes in This Book

Part 2 contains 100 traditional bread recipes that utilize a bread machine for all or part of the process. These recipes have been tested and tweaked to create the best possible appearance, texture, and flavor. You will find slender baguettes (page 82), rustic rye bread (page 74), golden buttery brioche (page 124), and everything in between for all your bread needs.

I have been making bread for decades and want to share with you the one fact that is true for all those years: Bread is never the same twice. Don't ever be discouraged by a loaf that is less than perfect—eat it anyway or use it for another recipe (see Leftover Bread Ideas, page 36). Try the recipe again another day. Myriad factors can change the results when baking bread. They can be environmental, such as humidity, ambient heat, or oven thermostat; ingredient related, such as expired yeast or a variation in measurements; or something that happens in the process including overproofing or underproofing the dough. As a chef, I am confident in the science behind ingredient combinations and processes, but I also know there is magic in the kitchen. I believe cooking with passion and a happy mood are reflected in the finished food, and bread is no different. So, approach each recipe as an adventure and enjoy the trip into the world of artisan bread.

Chapter One

ALL ABOUT BREAD

Understanding the Breadmaking Process

When you pick up a loaf of store-bought bread in its paper or plastic packaging, you might not realize the process that goes into its creation. Bread requires planning, time, and patience as well as chemical and biological reactions to produce a lovely tempting loaf. Every step has a purpose and skipping any one can mean disappointment in the end. Understanding the breadmaking process will give you an appreciation for the effort required to produce perfect loaves consistently. Some of these steps will occur in the bread machine, but many happen after removing the dough from the bucket. Here is the general breadmaking process:

Feeding the sourdough and making a pre-ferment: This step is only part of the process if you are making sourdough bread, or the recipe calls for a pre-ferment.

Mise en place: As with any culinary endeavor, read the recipe entirely so you know what you need and how long each part will take. It can be very frustrating to be excited about making bread, or anything else, only to find out the dough needs to rest overnight, or you don't have a crucial ingredient. *Mise en place* means "setting in place" in French and it is gathering your ingredients and tools. When I make bread or dough in the bread machine, I set everything I will need for the recipe on the counter and put the item back as I use it. This includes the bowls or baking sheet for later, kitchen cloth, and parchment paper.

Mixing: This process is a little different when using a bread machine for dough. In this case, you add the ingredients as recommended by your machine's manufacturer. I like to add the wet ingredients, at the appropriate temperatures, sugar, salt, and flavorings first, then the flour, spices, dry additives such as oats or seeds, and last, right on top, the yeast. Then, I program the machine for dough and let it do all the mixing, kneading, and first rise. However, if you were making bread the traditional way, you would mix your ingredients in a large bowl, sometimes activating the yeast in a smaller bowl with warm water and sugar. The recipe will usually guide you in the mixing order, often flour (or all dry ingredients except nuts, etc.) and liquid (all wet) first, then activated yeast or instant yeast. You are not kneading the dough at this point, just getting all the ingredients incorporated evenly.

Autolyse: This breadmaking step is optional and is often left out of recipes. Bread machine programs do include this step. Autolyse is covering the dough and letting it sit for about 30 minutes so the flour (gluten) can hydrate and the gluten network can start to form with no work from you. If the recipe is high in whole wheat flour, this step can make the dough softer and easier to handle.

WHAT IS GLUTEN?

Gluten is a protein found in cereal grains that creates the bread's structure, making it airy rather than crumbly like a cookie. Gluten is formed when two proteins in cereal grains, gliadin and glutenin, are mixed with water and bind together. When milled, the structure of the grain seed is destroyed but all its parts remain, including enzymes that cause the chemical reactions responsible for seed germination. When water is mixed with flour, the enzymes become active again and gluten development commences. As the dough is mixed, the protein chains multiply and become longer, creating a network that can hold its shape and expand. The longer the dough is worked, the stronger and more complex the gluten webbing becomes. Resting bread dough is often folded during the bulk fermentation phase to line the gluten strands into an organized structure that can trap the carbon dioxide produced by the yeast.

Gluten development can be checked using the windowpane test. This involves stretching a piece of dough between your fingers—if the dough can be pulled thin enough that it is translucent, the dough is developed enough to be formed into bread. The gluten development must be strong enough and sufficiently elastic to retain the gases produced during the proofing and baking process.

Factors that can influence gluten development include:

Fat: This ingredient can slow gluten production because it coats the proteins. This fat coating blocks hydration, so the proteins don't stick together as well, so the strands stay shorter. This is why enriched bread needs longer mixing times and has a tender crumb similar to cake.

Flour type: Different flours have different protein levels—11 percent to 13 percent is optimal—and, generally, higher protein means more gluten. Whole grain wheat flours contain sufficient protein, whereas semolina, rye, and other cereal grains need to be used as a blend because they do not form gluten effectively.

High-enzyme ingredients: Pineapple, papaya, and even too much milk can "kill" the gluten. Heating these ingredients to scalding, just under 212°F (100°C), can destroy the enzymes in them.

Salt: Gluten proteins actually repel each other, but the chlorine in the salt helps them stick together, which strengthens the gluten structure.

Sugar: Sugar naturally attaches to water molecules, so, in essence, it competes with the proteins in the flour. If too much sugar is present, the proteins cannot bind together effectively.

Water amount: Flour needs to be hydrated to wake up the proteins that form gluten. Too little or too much water will impede the creation of the gluten webbing.

Other factors can affect gluten development as well, such as mixing your doughs by hand or in a machine. Hand mixing does not hydrate the dough as effectively as using a machine, so gluten does not form as quickly.

HIGH-ALTITUDE CONSIDERATIONS

If you have never lived in an area with an elevation of 3,500 (1 km) feet or higher, you have never had to contend with the challenges of baking at high altitude. At higher elevations, air pressure is lower and the air is thinner and drier, so adjustments to your recipes are needed to ensure success. This climate means liquids evaporate faster and breads rise more quickly. Breads seem to rise beautifully, then fall flat. And you likely still have to bake on a trial-and-error basis. A recipe that works one day might fall flat the next, so don't give up. Adjust the recipes using one factor at a time to isolate what might be a problem in your microclimate and make a note when something works.

Some changes you can make to ensure your bread does not collapse at high altitude include:

- Decrease the yeast by 15 percent to 25 percent: Because the air is thinner at higher elevations, there is less resistance to the rise; this means breads can rise too fast, then collapse.

- Factor in shorter rise times, so give the bread an extra rise or slow the rise by refrigerating the dough: Chilling the dough slows the rising process.

- Increase the flour by 1 tablespoon (weight varies) at 3,500 feet and use a high-protein flour: This will improve the structure of the bread so it is not as prone to collapse.

- Increase the liquid by 2 to 3 tablespoons (30 to 45 ml) per 1 cup (weight varies) of flour: Evaporation happens faster in this climate; the air is drier, so increasing the liquid compensates for this factor.

- Increase the oven temperature by 15°F to 25°F (about 8°C to 15°C) and decrease the baking time by 20 percent to 25 percent: This should help set up the structure of the bread faster to combat the effects of rapid evaporation.

- Increase the salt by 1/8 to 1/4 teaspoon: Extra salt can impede the yeast, so the rise is not as swift.

- Make smaller loaves that require less proofing time to reduce overproofing: Less proofing time means less chance the bread will rise too fast and create large uneven pockets in the loaf, which then collapse.

- Use colder ingredients: This will slow the entire process, similar to refrigerating the dough. A slower rise means a better loaf in this scenario.

Kneading dough: If using a starter, add it at the end of the mixing step, or after autolyse. The point of kneading dough is to strengthen it and create the gluten network that will support the shape of the loaf. Kneading stretches the gluten, giving it form, and adds air to the dough. These air pockets fill with the gasses produced during fermentation, giving bread its desired light texture. If you read ten books on making bread, you might find ten techniques for kneading dough, including not kneading it at all. There is no set-in-stone correct method—do what works for you and the recipe you are creating. Some techniques recommend a combination of autolyse and slapping and folding the dough every 30 minutes. Some people like to knead with the heels of their hands in a push and turn method, similar to the technique your grandmother might have used. If making bread outside the bread machine, you will not add the salt until this stage of the process. So, add the salt after 15 minutes or so, or after the first fold, or when the recipe tells you it is time. As you can see, kneading can be complicated, which is why this book completes this step in the machine—no guesswork or mess required.

Bulk fermentation or first rise: When using a machine, this step happens in the bucket. When everything is mixed together, the gluten network is set, and the air is in the dough from kneading, you will now cover the dough and set it aside at room temperature for a quick rise, or in the refrigerator for a slow rise. The character and flavor of the bread will develop during this step—the longer it stretches, the more flavor that will develop. The yeast in the dough will eat the glucose from the flour and added sugars, converting it into energy. Carbon dioxide will form and the dough will expand and rise. This gas will fill the existing air pockets created by kneading. In the bread machine, the first rise is about 1 hour, but this step can take several hours, depending on the ambient temperature or the type of bread being made.

Stretch and fold: The dough's strength can be increased by folding the dough every 30 minutes. Depending on your kneading technique (skipping it completely after autolyse), the stretch and fold might completely replace kneading. Stretching the dough will create new pockets for the carbon dioxide to fill and relax the gluten. If you are using the French setting on your bread machine, you will notice the paddles will turn just one revolution every 20 minutes or so to degas the dough, mimicking this process.

Pre-shaping: After the first rise, transfer the dough to a lightly floured or oiled work surface and gently press it down to remove some of the gas. Be gentle; you don't want to flatten the dough completely—you want some room in the air pockets for the final rise. At this point, you can pre-shape the dough, but this is optional unless specified in the recipe. You will divide the dough, if dividing it, and shape the dough roughly into the finished form. Then, cover the dough and let it rest for about 20 minutes to relax the gluten.

Shaping: This step is crucial to the finished appearance of your loaf. Even if using the bread machine to complete the loaf, you should remove the proofed dough, take out the paddles, and shape the dough into a loaf before putting it back in the machine. With standard breadmaking, you will shape the rested dough firmly to create surface tension. You do not want to overwork your dough at this point, but don't be afraid to be assertive either. Different loaves will require different shaping techniques, and the various rolling, tucking, dragging, and smoothing steps are outlined in the recipe. You will see several shaping techniques illustrated on page 42 to help you visualize the methods.

Final proof: The shaped loaf will now rise again before baking, so it will need to be covered and set aside at room temperature. You may have created a free-form loaf on a baking sheet or tucked the dough into a loaf pan to proof. If you want a slow rise or to delay this step, refrigerate the shaped dough instead of leaving it at room temperature. You want the dough to rise without ruining the shape of the loaf, so if not on the baking sheet or in a pan, you can proof in a floured cloche or proofing basket. You can also use a medium-size bowl lined with a floured cloth (page 49) to mimic these specialty tools. Covering the loaf is crucial so that it does not dry out or form a skin, which will impede the rise that occurs while the loaf bakes.

Scoring: Scoring the dough will give the finished dough a traditional look, or you can create your own pattern. Scoring requires making shallow cuts in the top of the dough, either before the final rise or just before baking (the recipe will recommend the timing). Keep in mind that scoring the dough determines the direction the loaf expands in the oven. If you forget this step, you might find the sides of the loaf blown out. The cuts allow the dough to expand and rise.

Baking: So, several hours have passed, sometimes a day, depending on the recipe. It is time to bake your carefully crafted bread. Baking is a surprisingly complex process. It is in the oven that the bread will experience oven spring, a final expansion in size as the gases expand before the yeast is killed in the heat. The carbon dioxide will escape from its neat bubbles while the bread bakes. If your gluten network is strong and properly set, the bread will retain its shape and will not collapse as the gases release and the crust forms. You do not want the crust to set too early, or the final expansion will not occur, so the trick is using enough heat to cook the bread, evaporating the moisture, but not too much so the crust sets too early. Oven temperature will vary depending on the type of bread (sugar and fat content) and size of the loaf. If you bake a large loaf with high heat, you will end up with a dark crust before the inside of the bread is cooked. Bread will usually be done between 190°F and 210°F (88°C and 99°C).

Cooling: Whether using a bread machine or a conventional oven for baking your loaf, it is crucial to let the bread cool properly. Freshly baked bread smells heavenly, and it can be difficult not to cut into it immediately. However, you will have better bread if you place it on a raised wire rack to cool completely before cutting. See the note on page 114 and the section on cooling racks on page 50 for more.

Eating or storing: You probably don't need any direction on how to eat your bread. So, enjoy! However, storing bread can be tricky, depending on the type of bread and how much you need to set aside for another day. It goes without saying that fresh bread is best, and because homemade bread has no preservatives, you cannot keep it long sitting at room temperature. Here are some tips for storing both the dough and the finished bread:

Dough: Bread dough freezes beautifully but can be refrigerated for up to 3 days. If keeping it in the fridge, either place it in a lightly oiled bowl and cover it, or keep it in a sealed freezer bag. You will have to punch it down at least once a day because the yeast will be active even in that chilly environment. When ready to use the dough, take it out of the refrigerator, shape it, do the second rise, and bake. You can also freeze the dough in a sealed plastic bag for up to 3 months. The dough can be in a simple ball, or you can shape it into knots, braids, or loaves before freezing. When ready to use the frozen dough, thaw it completely in the refrigerator and follow the same steps as baking a chilled dough.

Freezing Bread

Freshly baked bread is best when consumed the day it is made, but this is sometimes impossible, especially when a recipe produces two or more loaves. So, the best solution is to freeze it. When freezing sandwich bread, slice the loaf before tucking it into a bag so you can remove slices as needed. Just cool completely and make sure you press out as much air as possible from the bag. Toast the bread straight from the freezer and, if making sandwiches to eat later, assemble them in the frozen bread slices, which will be thawed by the time you eat.

Baked bread: Most completely cooled bread can be stored in a sealed plastic bag at room temperature for at least 2 days, sometimes up to 5 days depending on the bread. Cooled bread can be frozen in a sealed freezer bag with the air pressed out for up to 2 months. Some sources say you can freeze bread for up to 6 months, but I find it can lose quality and texture if left that long. To thaw frozen bread, set it out at room temperature until thawed out.

GLUTEN-FREE FLOURS

The recipes in this book are not gluten free, although you can make many delicious loaves of bread in the bread machine and in the oven with gluten-free flours. Using single types of flour can be tricky because they do not react the same way to other ingredients as traditional bread flours. For example, coconut flour needs an incredible amount of liquid, and 100 percent almond flour can produce a crumbly bread.

The easiest method of creating gluten-free bread from standard recipes is to substitute a gluten-free flour blend 1:1 for wheat flour in the recipe. These store-bought blends are often designed for this substitution ratio, but you will probably have to experiment to get the correct taste and texture. Different blends will give you different flavor profiles, so read the label to get an idea of what a particular blend will produce. Ingredients are listed with the largest quantity first, in descending order to the ingredient that is in the smallest amount. So, if a blend has mostly almond flour, you can assume the flavor will reflect that. Here are some gluten-free flours you might find in a blend or want to try in your own recipes:

Almond flour: A sweet, nutritious flour that creates a tender crumb.

Amaranth flour: A high-fiber and -protein flour that can make bread dense because it absorbs a great deal of liquid.

Arrowroot: A very powdery flour not used in large quantities in blends; it has no flavor and can be used to lighten the texture of bread.

Bean flour: A very high-protein flour with a prominent bean taste; best used in bread that contains chocolate or other strong flavors to mask the taste.

Brown rice flour: A slightly nutty-tasting flour that can make bread gritty in texture.

Buckwheat: A popular flour in wheat-based breads for its distinct taste, which can also be delicious in gluten-free blends.

Cassava flour: A good neutral-tasting choice quite close to wheat flour in texture and fiber and often a significant ingredient in blends.

Chickpea flour: A more definite-tasting flour, which is not unpleasant; used in flatbreads because it is dense and effective when mixed with other flours.

Coconut flour: Absorbent flour with a delightful coconut taste, which needs to be combined with other flours or your bread will fall apart; make sure your blend is no more than 25 percent coconut flour; you must add extra liquid if this ingredient is present in the blend.

Millet flour: A nutty, pleasant-tasting flour that should be used in moderation—too much can give bread a coarse texture.

Potato starch: Most blends include this ingredient because it binds the other flours together.

Sorghum flour: Tastes similar to wheat flour; often used in gluten-free bread flour blends with success.

Teff flour: A nutritious high-protein flour that is mild tasting; commonly found in gluten-free flour blends.

Basic Ingredients

Basic bread is composed of very few ingredients—flour, water, yeast, and salt. Other ingredients can be added to this simple mixture to create texture, increase flavor, and boost the nutrition of the loaf, but you really only need the four to produce fabulous crusty loaves of freshly baked bread. Understanding the role each ingredient plays in the process can help you create better bread and adjust recipes if something is not quite right.

FLOUR

Flour is the main ingredient in bread, and this section covers wheat flours rather than gluten-free flours, which you can learn about on page 24. Wheat flour contains gluten-forming proteins called glutenins, which provide elasticity and strength, and gliadins, which give adhesive properties to the gluten. When water or a liquid is mixed with flour, these proteins hydrate and form gluten, the structural framework of bread. The proteins line up and form bonds creating long strands of gluten in a huge network throughout the dough. When you knead the dough, or use the fold and stretch method, the proteins interact and line up better, strengthening the gluten network. This gluten network traps the gas bubbles—carbon dioxide produced by the yeast. Flour also contains natural sugars that feed the yeast, allowing for fermentation and the production of these crucial gases.

The basic types of flour used in breadmaking are:

All-purpose flour: All-purpose flour, both bleached and unbleached, is the most common flour used to make bread, and either type will work fine. All-purpose flour in the United States has a gluten content of 9 percent to 11 percent and is made from both hard and soft wheats. It is milled to remove the bran and wheat germ, so it is very light and fluffy. If you are interested in the difference between unbleached and bleached, it comes down to aging. Unbleached flour is aged naturally to remove the wheat's yellow pigment and oxidize the proteins. It is more nutritious than bleached flour because the bleaching process with chlorine dioxide gas removes some nutrients. Most all-purpose flours are enriched, which means nutrients, such as B vitamins, iron, and calcium, are added after bleaching.

Bread flour: Bread flour is higher in protein than all-purpose flour, 11 percent to 14 percent. This is the protein percentage of Canadian all-purpose flour because this product is milled from 100 percent hard wheat. This higher protein percentage means more gluten, light-textured bread, and easy-to-handle dough. Bread flour requires more liquid to hydrate than all-purpose flour, so if you substitute all-purpose flour, add 1 tablespoon (15 ml) more liquid per cup (137 g) of bread flour.

White whole wheat flour: You might think this is just bleached whole wheat flour, but it is actually flour milled from white spring wheat, a sweet high-protein (12 percent) variety. You can substitute this nutritious flour for all-purpose and still have a lovely airy-textured bread.

Whole wheat flour: Look for 100 percent whole wheat flour to ensure the whole wheat berry is used, including the germ and bran. This flour is nutritious and has a pleasing nutty flavor. You can find both fine ground and coarse ground wheat flour, so pick the best one for your recipes. Coarse ground wheat will produce chewy loaves, and all-whole wheat flour creates a dense, heavy loaf. This product has about 16 percent gluten content, so you might wonder why the loaves do not rise as quickly as bread made with a

lower-gluten flour. Basically, whole wheat flour contains bits of the hull that can cut the gluten strands, so they do not form an extensive gluten network.

WATER

Water is often overlooked in the breadmaking process—the quality and amount a second thought after flour and yeast. Generally, the water content of bread ranges from 60 percent to 85 percent of the flour weight. The higher the water content, the larger the holes and looser the structure: Think ciabatta bread. The type of water used can affect the fermentation of the yeast. Very hard water contains yeast action–retarding magnesium sulfate, so this dough will require more time to rise. Hard water also tends to be alkaline, and yeast likes an acidic environment. Once the yeast starts to work in the alkaline dough, the mineral salts and pH create a firmer dough because the gluten will be tighter. Water is crucial to bread success, and it has many functions in the process. For example:

- Water activates yeast.
- When combined with flour, water forms gluten.
- It dissolves the other ingredients, such as salt and sugar.
- Water hydrates the dough, sticking the ingredients together.
- Water evenly disperses the yeast throughout the dough.
- It can help stabilize and control the temperature of the dough, which is crucial for yeast survival.

WHAT IS WILD YEAST?

If you are new to breadmaking, your experience with yeast might consist of those small packages and jars of tiny yeast granules you find in the baking section of the grocery store. This product comes in traditional, dry active, quick-rising, and bread machine varieties and is the yeast found in the majority of recipes in this book.

So, how did ancient civilizations leaven their bread thousands of years ago if yeast wasn't commercially cultivated and packaged until the turn of the twentieth century? The answer lies all around you—wild yeast. These fungi are everywhere—in your house, the garden, trees, your car, and wherever else you touch, including your entire body from the crown of your head to your toes. Appealing thought, isn't it? In ancient times, all the way up to about 150 years ago, wild yeast was gathered and kept alive in a flour and water mixture by feeding it every day with more water and flour. This starter, which could live for years, was used to make delicious bread back before commercial yeast was available.

You can collect your own wild yeast to make some of the starters needed for sourdough bread and other recipes. It is simple but can take a great deal of time and a bit of effort. You can find the method to create a wild yeast starter on page 106.

So, why would anyone bother with this when you can open a package and use those handy little granules to make bread—and a starter for that matter? Wild yeast produces wonderful bread that does not create the digestive upheaval associated with gluten. Most people with gluten sensitivities can eat traditional wild yeast starter–sourdough bread with no issues. You will have to let dough made with wild yeast rise longer, as much as 6 hours, but this extra time is when the *lactobacilli* bacteria in the yeast cultures change gluten and other proteins into lactic acid. During this long rise, the wild yeast also breaks down the anti-nutrients in the grain (flour).

Grains do not break down easily because they contain anti-nutrients such as gluten and phytic acid, which block the absorption of nutrients. This is why you can store grains (and flour) for so long without rancidity or loss in quality. Store-bought yeast does not break down the anti-nutrients because it is only the active ingredient of yeast, not the full fungi. Full-fungi yeast feeds on the natural sugars found in grain converting this food source into the carbon dioxide that gives the rise in bread. Traditional wild yeast bread does not have added sugar or sweeteners, so the yeast is forced to feed off the grain itself, creating a bread that is easier to digest.

YEAST

Yeast can be intimidating; it is often the reason people do not make bread at home. Who wants to mess with an ingredient that is alive? There are thousands of these single-cell microorganisms in one little package of yeast, and they make the dough rise and gives it the distinctive "bread" taste and enticing aroma. When yeast is activated by water, it releases an enzyme that converts sucrose to dextrose, which is then broken down into carbon dioxide. This gas gets trapped in the gluten network in the dough, making the dough rise. As bread bakes, these carbon dioxide bubbles expand, creating texture and airiness in the bread.

There are many types of yeast to choose from in the store, and they are not usually interchangeable. Four common types of yeast are:

Active dry yeast: Most bread recipes use this type of yeast, *other than in a bread machine*. This yeast is dehydrated and made inert before being put into jars or packages, so it requires proofing—mixing with water—before combining it with other ingredients. Often a sprinkle of sugar is added to the water and yeast mixture to accelerate the yeast's growth. This type of yeast is not used in the majority of recipes in this book because the bread machine does not proof its yeast; this ingredient is added to the top of the flour to avoid contact with the salt at the bottom (see Salt, at right).

Cake or compressed yeast: This type of yeast is not used in recipes in this book, but it can be very useful because it produces more gases than the other types of yeast. Cake yeast is alive and highly perishable, so keep it refrigerated for up to 2 weeks. Healthy cake yeast has a creamy texture, and you can break it cleanly.

Instant dry yeast: This yeast is milled finer than active dry yeast, so it can be added directly to dry ingredients, making it an excellent choice for the recipes in this book. Instant dry yeast will speed the rise, cutting the required time in half. Using instant dry yeast often means you can go directly from the first rise to shaping the loaf. This can decrease the flavor of the bread, but it is very convenient.

Rapid rise yeast or bread machine yeast: As the name implies, this yeast will accelerate the rise of your dough, sometimes cutting the time in half. The yeast granules are ground smaller than standard yeast, so this type does not require proofing.

Here are a few facts to remember about yeast:

- Yeast needs a controlled temperature to thrive—too cold and it will be sluggish; too hot and it will die. Keep the liquids used between 100°F and 110°F (38°C and 43°C).
- Yeast feeds on sugar to grow, either natural sugars in flour or added sugar.
- A warm kitchen, 70°F to 80°F (21°C to 27°C), enables the yeast to feed and the bread to rise.
- Refrigerate or freeze your yeast to keep it fresh and check the expiration date to ensure your yeast is active.
- Yeast becomes dormant in cold temperatures, so you can freeze the finished dough and it will stop rising. When you want to bake the bread or rolls, leave the dough at room temperature to thaw and the yeast will wake up and rise again.

SALT

There are very few breads that do not contain salt; only Tuscan bread (page 93) in this book. Obviously, salt adds flavor to bread, even sweet bread where a bit of salt enhances the sweet flavor. Salt has many other roles in breadmaking besides improving taste. Salt slows the fermentation process and controls the yeast action. This means your dough won't rise too much or too fast, then collapse. One essential rule of breadmaking is to keep the salt away from the yeast—it is usually added to the flour, about 1 teaspoon per 4 cups (weight varies) of flour. This is why salt is added to the liquids in the bread machine, and the yeast is placed on top of the flour. Salt also enhances gluten development, creating a stronger, more stable network. Fine table salt and fine sea salt work best in dough because they dissolve easily. Coarse salt or flaky coarse sea salt should be saved for finishing breads—just sprinkle a little on the top of the dough before baking, for a lovely flavor and savory crunch.

FATS AND OILS

Almost any type of fat or oil, such as butter, olive oil, vegetable oils, margarine, nut oils, and shortening, can be used in bread recipes. Fat improves the texture of the bread and enhances the taste. Generally, the more fat in the bread, the softer the texture and the greater the volume of the loaf. Fat lubricates the other ingredients, softening the gluten, and allows the ingredients to slide easily over each other improving the rise. Larger amounts of fat, such as in brioche, will also form a thin layer on the yeast molecules impeding the release of gases, slowing fermentation and rise. Fat, similar to sugar, can stop moisture from evaporating from your baked bread, so it will stay fresh longer. If your recipe calls for a solid fat such as margarine or shortening and you use a liquid oil instead, grease your loaf pan or baking tray because the oil will be absorbed into the dough and the bread might stick to the pan.

SUGAR

It should be no surprise that sugar adds flavor and color (through caramelization, or the Maillard reaction) to bread, but it also serves as food for the yeast. Yeast eats the sugar and produces carbon dioxide and alcohol, which create a rise in bread. Sometimes the sugar comes from the flour, and sometimes it is added in the form of granulated sugar, brown sugar, honey, maple syrup, or molasses. Flour is 2 percent to 3 percent sugar, sucrose, and maltose, which is just enough to jump-start fermentation, but not enough for the final rise. So additional sugar is required to complete the process. A little sugar in a recipe, less than ¼ cup (50 g), will increase fermentation and rise, but larger quantities, such as 1 cup (200 g), will stop it. Sugar attaches to water molecules, so it will compete with the proteins in the flour, impeding the formation of gluten. This is why sweet breads usually need a longer

rise. This attraction to moisture means sugar can also act as a preservative, preventing baked bread from going stale quickly and hardening. If you replace granulated sugar with liquid sugar, remember to count this amount in your liquid amounts.

EGGS

Eggs are used to add richness, color, light texture, protein, and fat to doughs. Think of your favorite tender sweet bread, such as brioche (page 124) or challah (page 127), and you will see the influence of eggs. The protein in the eggs can tighten the gluten. So, where eggs are used, there is also usually fat in the recipe to counter the effect. Eggs, blended with water, are also used as a wash to create a tender golden crust. Remember that eggs are part of the liquid amount in a bread recipe, so if you want to add one to an eggless recipe, account for the amount. For example, if the recipe calls for 1½ cups (360 ml) milk (water or other liquid),

crack the egg into the measuring cup, then add the liquid so it equals 1½ cups (360 ml).

DAIRY

Dairy, such as milk, buttermilk, sour cream, cheeses, and butter, which is considered a fat, is a common ingredient in bread recipes. Milk comes a close second, after water, for liquids in bread because this ingredient can create soft, moist, white bread with a lovely rich flavor. Unlike water, milk adds protein to the bread, which can tighten the gluten. If you do not want this effect, scald the milk to neutralize the enzymes and cool it before using. Milk can also produce a gorgeous golden crust because milk sugar caramelizes at the end of baking, as yeast cannot ferment this type of sugar. Other dairy products are usually used to add flavor and tenderness to bread and are considered liquids in the recipe.

Extra Ingredients

Other than the basic ingredients, the flavor and texture of bread can be enhanced with an assortment of other ingredients. Be careful with the volume of ingredients added and the timing of when you add them to the bread dough because some can impede the action of the yeast or create a very dense dough. Some extra ingredients to add to your bread include:

CHEESE

Who doesn't like cheese bread? This tempting ingredient is a wonderful addition to artisan bread recipes, whether made in the bread machine or baked in a conventional oven. You can add grated cheese or small chunks, or simply sprinkle the cheese on the surface of the bread. Some things to consider when adding cheese are:

- If using a salty cheese, reduce the salt in the recipe.
- Hard cheese is best grated rather than added as larger cubes because it will not melt; if using cubed cheese, cut the cheese into ¼-inch (6 mm) pieces.
- Hard cheeses should be used in smaller amounts because they have a strong flavor.
- Softer cheeses, such as Cheddar, Swiss, and mozzarella, can be grated or cubed. Cubes should be ¼ to ½ inch (0.6 to 1 cm).
- Creamy cheeses, such as cream cheese and mascarpone, can be added during the kneading process and will blend right into the dough.

- Make sure the cheese is at room temperature.
- Follow the recipe directions concerning when to incorporating the cheese. Most cheeses are added to the liquids, before the flour, especially soft cheeses, because they add liquid to the dough.
- If the dough looks too sticky and wet, add a few tablespoons of flour.
- A coarse shred of cheese will add both flavor and color to your bread.
- Cubes of cheese will create a hole in the loaf about the size of the cube.
- Shredded cheese can be sprinkled on the dough and baked. Don't use too much, or the bread will end up greasy.

CHOCOLATE

Chocolate can be used in both sweet and savory breads. This refers to real chocolate rather than cocoa powder. White, milk, semi-sweet, and dark chocolate can be grated into the dough or added as chips after kneading or the first rise.

CITRUS ZEST

Fresh or candied zest or peel (page 129) can add an incredible burst of flavor to bread and is the main ingredient in some traditional loaves, such as panettone. If adding fresh zest, toss it in with the liquid ingredients or the flour. If adding larger chunks of candied peel, put it in when the machine signals, or at the second kneading.

Most bread machines have a beep or some sort of signal to indicate when the first kneading cycle is complete. That is the time to add ingredients such as nuts, fruit, cheese, and seeds.

COCOA POWDER

You will find unsweetened cocoa powder in many dark bread recipes, such as pumpernickel (page 73) and Russian black bread (page 67). This ingredient adds a gorgeous bitterness and dark color to the bread. If the bread's sugar content is higher, the bread will taste like dark chocolate.

COCONUT

No recipe in this book includes coconut, but it can be a delicious addition to sweet bread and will add texture to whole grain or oatmeal bread. Use sweetened or unsweetened coconut, which is grated, flaked, and shredded.

COFFEE

This ingredient can be added as a liquid or as espresso powder for flavor. You can replace the water in a recipe with brewed coffee, depending on the bread. Coffee also adds depth of flavor to dark rye and black breads.

EXTRACTS

These intense flavorings are used in moderation in breads, especially sweet breads, where a little vanilla or almond extract boosts the taste. Add this ingredient with the liquids.

FRUIT

Dried and fresh fruits are bursts of flavor in bread. Fresh fruit can be cut into chunks; added whole, such as with blueberries; or as a purée, like pumpkin and apple. Sometimes extra flour needs to be added to offset the juice in the fruit. Dried fruit can include apples, apricots, cranberries, dates, figs, and raisins added when the machine signals, or in the second kneading cycle in a bread machine.

HERBS

Fresh and dried herbs are common ingredients in bread because they add flavor and do not affect the rise or texture of the bread. Try basil, chives, dill, oregano, rosemary, or thyme to enhance different breads, such as baguettes or cheese bread.

NUTS

You will find many recipes that include chopped or ground nuts. Nuts add a lovely crunch and delightful flavor. They are usually added when the bread machine signals, or after the kneading cycle is complete. Try almonds, cashews, hazelnuts, pecans, pine nuts, pistachios, and walnuts for different taste profiles.

OLIVES

Any type of olive can be used in bread—from green to brown to deep black. Olives can be added sliced or chopped when the machine signals, or placed on top of bread like focaccia (page 150). Olives are moist, so they will alter the texture of the bread slightly. They are also salty, so you might need to adjust the salt.

SEEDS

What would bread be without seeds? Many bread recipes include seeds in the bread or scattered on top for a beautiful presentation. Seeds can be added with the flour and, usually, do not affect the rise. For extra crunch and complex flavor, try caraway seeds, chia seeds, flaxseed, fennel seeds, poppy seeds, pumpkin seeds, sesame seeds, and sunflower seeds.

SKIM MILK POWDER

A couple tablespoons of skim milk powder add sweetness and tenderness to the interior of the bread and can help create a golden crust.

SPICES

Dried spices can enhance the flavor of many bread types, both sweet and savory. Spices are very potent, so use them in moderation. Try anise, cardamom, cinnamon, cloves, coriander, cumin, nutmeg, and saffron threads in your recipes, added to the flour.

VEGETABLES

Potatoes, sweet potato, beets, carrots, and other vegetables can create a gloriously soft texture in bread or add sweetness or intense color, in the case of beets and carrots. These vegetables are usually added to the liquids, either puréed or grated.

VITAL WHEAT GLUTEN

Extra gluten added to dense loaves or bread filled with dried fruit or nuts can ensure a satisfactory rise. If you add vital wheat gluten, add an equivalent amount of liquid, too.

A Sprinkle of Sesame

Sesame seeds are a very common topping for bread, found on crusty loaves and hamburger buns alike, because they add a lovely crunch and look pretty. Sesame seeds come in yellow, white, black, and red, so try any color you prefer, even all for a spectacular finish. Make sure the seeds you purchase come in sealed containers with no evident moisture. Sesame seeds have a high oil content, so they can get rancid. Refrigerate or freeze them to maintain freshness.

WHOLE GRAINS

Rolled oats, cooked farro, bulgur, quinoa, and other grains are incredible in bread—they add taste, texture, and nutrition to the finished loaf. Some are added cooked and some raw, so follow the recipe or use common sense with these additions. If a grain needs to be cooked to be soft enough to eat, then cook it before adding it to the bread.

LEFTOVER BREAD IDEAS

Despite the fact that freshly baked bread is incredible, you may find yourself with leftover pieces—or whole loaves if you go on a baking binge. You can certainly freeze bread when it is fresh, but what about those stale pieces that seem to accumulate in the breadbox? Luckily, there are many uses and recipes for leftover bread. Here are some ideas worth trying:

Bread crumbs

This is probably the most straightforward use of leftover bread. Wait until the bread is hard, then pulse in a food processor until fine or coarse crumbs form. Freeze the bread crumbs in an airtight container or sealed plastic bag for up to 3 months. Use them for toppings, meatballs or meatloaf, sauces, and dips.

Bread pudding

One of the most decadent desserts you can make is egg- and sugar-infused bread pudding. The variations are endless—apple, banana nut, caramel, chocolate, pumpkin, and vanilla. Stale bread is the base of this dessert, and you will need at least one loaf for a recipe. A 1-pound (454 g) loaf (most loaves are 1 pound, or 454 g) yields about 10 cups (454 g) of cubes, which is about right for a bread pudding. If you don't have that much, cut the stale bread into cubes and freeze in a sealed bag until you can collect enough.

Bruschetta

Slices of stale bread are the ideal base for this tomato, herb, garlic, and oil topping. Either make your own bruschetta mixture, taking care to strain the tomatoes so they don't make the bread soggy, or purchase a store-bought mixture. Top the bread with the bruschetta mixture and cheese, if using, and bake until sizzling. Delicious!

Crostini

These crisp little slices of bread are perfect for serving as appetizers, dunking in tempting dips, or topping a steaming bowl of onion soup. Thinly slice leftover bread—a baguette is best—and bake the slices in a low-heat oven until dried and crispy. Freeze the crostini in an airtight container for up to 3 months.

Croutons

Cut stale bread slices into cubes and either immediately bake them with a little oil and seasonings, such as garlic or herbs, or freeze the cubes in a sealed bag until you have enough for baking a tray full of croutons. Store in a sealed container at room temperature for up to 1 week.

Fondue

This charming dish from the 1970s and '80s had everyone dipping chunks of stale bread into bubbling, stretchy, melted cheese, but it has gone out of fashion. Some fine-dining restaurants have brought back fondue as a kitschy way to spend the evening, so why not have a fondue party at home? Simply cut the bread into 1-inch (2.5 cm) cubes and serve them with melted cheese.

French toast

Who doesn't love thick-sliced bread soaked in egg and fried to a delectable golden brown? French toast can be assembled in a casserole dish and baked as well. The best bread for this scrumptious dish is brioche or some type of enriched bread, but any will do in a pinch.

Panzanella salad

This traditional Tuscan salad is made with stale bread cubes, tomatoes, onion, cucumber, and fresh herbs soaked in a simple oil and vinegar dressing.

Strata

Strata is a baked casserole layered with eggs, vegetables, meats, herbs, cheese, and, of course, stale bread cubes. This mixture of delicious ingredients sits overnight, or at least a few hours, so the bread can soak up the beaten egg. It is, basically, a savory bread pudding. A standard strata requires ten to twelve slices of bread.

Chapter Two

MAKING ARTISAN BREAD USING A BREAD MACHINE

How a Bread Machine Works

Bread machines are not new inventions, even though the small models used now cropped up in 1986 when appliance companies started manufacturing them for baking single loaves in the comfort of your own home. The earliest mechanical breadmaking machine was invented by Sarah Stearns in California, U.S.A., and patented in 1903. This machine did not bake the bread and still required the operator to crank handles that powered rollers that kneaded dough. It was, basically, a kneading machine, but when used in bakeries that produced hundreds of loaves, the labor and time saved using this machine were substantial. Obviously, bread machines have evolved for both commercial ventures and home use over the years.

As with many other things in life, you don't need to know precisely how a bread machine works to reap the benefits of using one. Bread machines are convenient, and the bread they produce is delicious and often identical to bread prepared by hand. Using the machine for even a portion of the breadmaking process saves a great deal of effort and time. So, for those who like to know everything, how does this boxy bread machine work?

For the sake of comprehensive information, the process described here will be for creating bread from start to finish in the machine, even though for the purposes of this book, most recipes use only the dough program. Generally, a bread machine does similar tasks to what a person making bread would do—without all the mixing, kneading, and mess. The only thought that has to go into a loaf of bread made entirely in the machine is the amount and order of ingredients. Follow the recipes carefully, or the manufacturer's recommended order of ingredients, for best results. For example, don't mix yeast with salt in the liquid ingredients, or your results will not be as intended (or expected!).

When the ingredients are layered into the bread machine's bucket, select the program you want to run, the size of the loaf, if applicable, and the browning level on the crust. Different machines come with various programs that have individual timing but usually follow the same sequence of cycles. After selecting the program, press Start and walk away. Well, don't really walk away. I can't help but watch the mixing and kneading cycles, sometimes with a glass of wine, like it is a TV program! The machine mixes the ingredients for 2 to 4 minutes with the paddles, then most machines let the dough rest for 10 to 15 minutes to mimic autolyse (page 18). Then the kneading will commence, with the paddles turning one way, then the opposite way, for about 25 minutes. You can watch the dough come together and become elastic and uniform in texture. If the dough seems dry or wet, you can adjust it with either more liquid or flour, as needed. Do not be afraid to pop open the lid on the machine. During the kneading cycle, there might be a signal about 10 minutes in signaling to add any extra ingredients, such as butter for brioche or nuts and raisins.

When the kneading cycle is complete, the bulk fermentation process, or first rise, begins. During this cycle the thermostat in the machine will raise the temperature slightly to an optimal level for this process to occur. The bulk fermentation cycle lasts about 1 hour, 15 minutes with a "punch down" at about 40 minutes with a few turns of the paddles.

If you are baking the bread entirely in the machine, remove the paddles and shape the dough when the cycle is finished, so the bread is uniform and doesn't have huge holes in the bottom.

If using the dough program, remove the dough after this cycle is complete and proceed with the recipe.

If baking the bread in the machine, a second rise occurs similar to the final proof of loaves after shaping and before baking.

The baking cycle is now ready to start. The programming in the machine will raise the temperature to the level associated with the program, size of the loaf, and browning level selected. Most baking cycles take between 50 and 60 minutes. There will be a signal, the machine will shut off, and your bread is done! I like to remove the bucket from the machine right away because the heat in the machine can stay elevated for 15 to 20 minutes after the machine turns off. This would be similar to leaving the loaf in the oven after turning off the oven. Remove the bread from the bucket and let cool completely before slicing.

Layer the ingredients in the bucket: liquids, sweetener, and salt at the bottom; flour and yeast on the top.

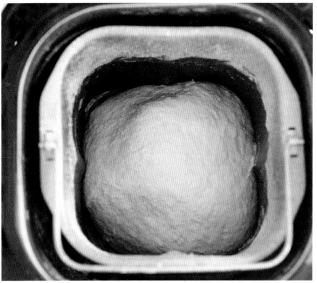

The Dough cycle finished and the dough ready to be removed and shaped for the rise or left in the machine to rise and bake.

Shaping Dough

Some of the recipes in this book use the bread machine to mix the ingredients and form the dough. Then the dough is removed from the machine, shaped, and baked in the oven. Below are the most common shaping techniques you'll use.

Shape dough into a ball by tucking the edges under and dragging it toward you, creating tension. Repeat this process of dragging on all sides to create a smooth, perfect surface.

Dough can be divided and formed into any size or shape depending on your preference. One batch of dough can yield a single large loaf, two medium loaves, or several small dough balls, which are perfect for buns.

To create a baguette, stretch and fold the dough into a long stick, then roll it on a lightly floured surface to achieve the traditional baguette shape. Remember: They do not have to be perfect!

Slashing the dough ensures that the folds and layers you have created will expand through the slash, creating the signature baguette look.

WHY MEASURING MATTERS

Cooking is an art, but baking is a science, so precision is crucial to recipe success. When making bread, you can undoubtedly indulge your creativity by adding a pinch of this and a dash of that concerning spices and other additions, but base ingredient amounts, such as flour, need to be spot-on. A slight deviation in quantities of flour, water, or salt can produce considerable changes in the finished loaf. After reading a recipe and gathering the ingredients, the first step is measuring everything.

You can measure by either weight or volume. This book uses volume (with weight in parentheses) because most people have a set of measuring cups in their kitchen—but weight is more accurate. When measuring by volume, be as meticulous as possible and use the correct measuring cup. You might be unaware that both liquid and dry measuring cups exist and may only have one type, which you use for everything. Liquid measuring cups are see-through glass or plastic, and their measurement lines do not come right to the top. When you pour in liquid, you can see exactly what the measure is, and the extra room at the top of the cup prevents spills. Dry measuring cups are meant to be slightly overfilled and leveled off, meaning the top of the cup is the measurement line.

To measure liquids: Place the cup on the counter or a level surface and fill it to the measurement line you require, using the top of the curved surface of the liquid as the guide. This curvature is called the meniscus. Make sure you bend down and look at the line at eye level so the reading is accurate.

To measure dry ingredients: Measuring dry ingredients, especially flour, is slightly trickier and you might find you have been doing it wrong up to now. How many times have you scooped flour with the measuring cup directly from the bag, then shaken or tapped it so the surface is relatively flat? This method can pack the flour into the cup too tightly and the resulting amount will be more than required for the recipe—sometimes as much as 25 percent more in each cup.

The best way to measure flour is to stir it in the bag first so it is light and unsettled. Then use a spoon to fill the correct measuring cup (1 cup, 1/2 cup, or other amount) so the flour is higher than the top. Sweep the back of a knife or other flat edge across the cup to level off the flour precisely. Other ingredients such as sugar, cocoa powder, and shredded coconut can be measured this way as well. You will get much better results with your finished breads and other baked products by measuring ingredients correctly.

Bread Machine Cycles

Bread machines have come a long way since the original models and offer an assortment of cycles for all your set-it-and-forget-it breadmaking needs. The majority of recipes in this book, about 75 percent, do not utilize any program other than the Dough setting, but it is nice to know you can complete your loaves in the machine using the appropriate programming. Most machines have similar cycles, although there can be variations among models and price ranges. Generally, the bread machine cycles are:

Bagel Dough: This is not a programmed cycle on every type of machine. It is similar to the Dough cycle. You remove the finished dough, shape it, do the second rise, boil, and bake as with all bagels.

Basic/White Bread: You likely will use this cycle the most because it is versatile and handles most recipes with white flour and recipes that include about 25 percent whole wheat, rye, or oat flour. The cycle is between 3 and 4 hours, depending on the size of the loaf and browning level.

Delay or Timed Bake: Most machines have the option of timing the start of the cycle. Basically, you place the ingredients in the bucket and program the machine to start at a certain time. This is convenient if you want fresh bread when you walk in the door at the end of the day. Do not delay the bake cycle for more than 1 hour for recipes that include perishable ingredients such as milk, eggs, cheese, or butter.

Dough: This is the most crucial bread machine cycle for this book. You will use it to make about three-quarters of the bread dough recipes. The cycle handles the kneading and first rise. When signaled, remove the dough and continue the breadmaking process with the formed loaf in the oven. You avoid a great deal of the work and mess when making the bread dough in the machine's bucket.

French: This is one of the longer cycles available in a bread machine, designed to create the harder crusts found on French and Italian breads. The rise times are longer and the baking temperature higher than the Basic cycle.

Gluten-Free: Gluten-free bread is very different from "regular" bread—there is a shorter rise time and the bread has a different texture than yeasted wheat bread.

Jam: This cycle turns the bread machine bucket into a saucepan—just add diced fruit. The bucket gets very hot, and the fruit cooks for about 1½ hours. Be very careful removing the bucket from the machine so you do not burn yourself.

Quick Bread: Quick breads include non-yeast breads, such as banana bread, and they do not need time to rise, so the program is shorter by about 2 hours. The ingredients are mixed and baked with baking powder and baking soda, creating the texture and lift.

Rapid/Quick Bake: Some bread machine recipes specify a rapid or quick cycle, although none in this book has this label. The rise time is shortened, or there is just one proof, so the entire cycle can be 45 minutes to 2 hours less than the basic cycle.

Sweet: Recipes that include eggs or have higher fat and sugar content, basically enriched yeast bread, require a lower baking temperature so the crust does not burn or become too dark. The sweet cycle is perfect for brioche (page 124) or challah (page 127) because the machine signals after the first kneading and you can add the butter at this point.

Whole Wheat/Whole Grain: This cycle has more extended kneading and rising times built in to handle whole wheat and whole grain recipes to ensure the finished bread has the correct texture and a good height. The whole wheat dough needs a longer rise so the gluten has time to work. If you add vital wheat gluten to the dough, you can use the Basic cycle.

How to Choose a Bread Machine

You might already have a bread machine and want to expand the type of bread you create with this handy tool, or have picked up this book because you want to start making bread. No matter the reason, you will need a bread machine. There are many bread machines on the market—a dizzying array of choices that can seem confusing. I am not going to go through the various brands because the selection might change depending on where you live in the world. It is better to consider other factors to pick the best bread machine for your needs.

Price: This one factor might be the overriding determinant in your purchasing decision. Bread machines can range from $50 to $300 and more. Generally, the more expensive, the more options, but you can get an excellent durable machine for about $100. The only feature you need to use this book effectively is the Dough cycle.

Size of loaves: The loaf size on bread machines is measured in pounds, and the recipes in this book are for 2-pound (908 g) programs. Think about how much bread you want to make. If you are feeding two or three people, 3-pound (1.36 kg) loaves might be too large. Homemade bread does not have the preservatives that store-bought bread contains, so it will become stale quickly unless eaten or frozen. If you want flexibility in loaf size, some machines have three or more choices. The size of your kitchen might also be a determining factor—bread machines are large and need either counter space or cupboard space.

Kneading paddles: You would think kneading paddles would be standard across the various machines, but they come in different shapes and numbers. Some machines have only one paddle but, if you are using this tool for dough, you want two paddles. Double paddles knead the dough as effectively as kneading by hand, or even some mixers. I find removable paddles make cleaning the bucket easier, and you have the option to take them out before the bake cycle starts, if finishing the bread in the machine. You don't have to take the paddles out, but leaving them in creates holes in the bottom of the loaf.

Delayed timer: Most mid-price machines have a timer so you can start the programs when convenient. Do you want freshly baked bread when you wake up in the morning? No problem—just set the time and the machine does the rest. Most machines that include this feature have a 12-hour programming window. If you are using the bread maker only for dough, this option will not be as important.

Noise: Bread machines can be noisy during the kneading cycle, and if the model is not sturdy, it can actually shake so much it ends up moving right off the counter! Look at the mid-price models made of quality materials to avoid too much disturbance.

Alarm: Another feature that can be noisy is the alarm, which signals the time for adding fruit, nuts, and other ingredients. This is an

How to Convert 2-Pound (908 g) Bread Machine Recipes to Different Sizes

Most recipes in this book made from start to finish in the bread machine stipulate 2-pound (908 g) settings. So, how do you make the recipe if you have a machine that is either smaller or larger? You do a little math. You will use the following equations on each ingredient in the recipe for the new size. If the calculation comes up with a less common measurement, round up or down to the nearest logical amount. For example, ⅞ teaspoon would be 1 teaspoon.

Convert from 2 pounds (908 g) to 1 pound (454 g): divide by 2

Convert from 2 pounds (908 g) to 1½ pounds (681 g): multiply by 0.75

Convert from 2 pounds (908 g) to 2½ pounds (1.1 kg): multiply by 1.25

Convert from 2 pounds (908 g) to 3 pounds (1.36 kg): multiply by 1.5

extremely convenient feature because adding these ingredients earlier means they can get crushed in the kneading cycles. If you do not have this option, you will have to oversee the process to determine precisely when the first kneading cycle ends.

WHY USE A THERMOMETER?

I didn't start using an instant-read digital thermometer for breadmaking until a few years ago, and the positive difference it makes in results is huge. Do you have to incorporate this tool into your breadmaking? Certainly not, but here are the ways it can help the process.

Use it to measure the temperature of liquid ingredients. Yeast is most active between 100°F and 110°F (38°C and 43°C), so you can make sure the liquids aren't too hot or cold right from the start.

Many bread books tell you to tap the bottom of the baked loaf for doneness, looking for a hollow sound. This can be a good indicator, but picking up a loaf of bread in a hot oven to thump the bottom can be a dangerous venture resulting in scorched fingers or wrists. Instead, insert a thermometer and instantly know if the loaf is ready.

Most bread and rolls need an internal temperature of 190°F (88°C), and enriched bread 200°F (93°C). However, you will also see higher internal temperatures of 210°F (99°C) for baguettes and some denser breads, such as rye loaves. If you are making gluten-free bread, bake to 205°F (96°C) to provide structure to the bread. High-altitude baking requires dropping all the temperatures by 5°F (2°C) because water has a lower boiling point at higher altitudes.

No matter the recommendation, a thermometer is the most accurate and easiest method to ensure perfectly baked bread.

Specialty programs: Beyond the basic programs, such as White Bread, Whole Wheat/Whole Grain, Sweet, Rapid Bake, and French, there can also be settings for Quick Bread, Jam, and Gluten-Free. You might end up with these options even if you do not need them, depending on the other factors relevant to you.

Removable bread bucket: Most bread machines have removable buckets. The option to remove the bucket makes removing the finished loaf simple—just tip it out. And, cleaning the bucket is a snap if you can put it in the dishwasher or wash it in the sink.

Other Tools You Will Need

Some tools listed here are needed both for making bread in a machine and finishing the breadmaking process in the oven. Read the recipe you wish to make to determine if you have the tools needed for each step. Most recipes in this book do not require any specialty items, so your kitchen is probably more than adequately outfitted. If you do not have all the tools, add these items as you continue your breadmaking journey.

Baking sheets: Baking sheets should be heavy-gauge aluminum to withstand high temperatures. The dimensions of the baking sheets you purchase will depend on the size of your oven. Good choices include 10½ × 15-inch (26 × 38 cm) or 11 × 17-inch (28 × 43 cm) or 9½ × 12½-inch (24 × 31 cm) baking sheets.

Bench/bowl scraper: This tool is a flexible rectangle used to lift and fold doughs, scrape the work surface, cut dough into pieces, and scrape the dough out of the bowl.

Dutch oven: This heavy pot has a tight-fitting lid and is usually made from cast iron, either enamel coated or plain. This vessel can withstand very high heat and is perfect for several recipes in this book. Look for a 5½-quart (5.2 l) enameled cast-iron Dutch oven for breadmaking.

Kitchen towels/plastic wrap: Dough needs to be covered while rising, so you will need sizable clean kitchen towels and plastic wrap. Sometimes these tools will be used alone or together, depending on the recipe.

Knives: You probably have knives in your kitchen, which you will need for breadmaking. A sharp knife is required to slash the top of the dough, and a serrated knife will cut your baked bread perfectly without squishing the loaf.

Loaf pans: Several recipes in this book use 9 × 5-inch (23 × 13 cm) loaf pans to create perfect bread for standard sandwiches. Look for heavy-gauge nonstick aluminum pans for best results. The finish should be dull rather than shiny, which can create an overdone crust. You can also use an 8½ × 4½-inch (21 × 11 cm) loaf pan.

Measuring cups and spoons: You will need these tools for both bread machine–finished bread and oven-finished bread. Get both liquid and dry measuring cups and a set of measuring spoons to cover all your needs.

Mixing bowls: You will need bowls for proofing dough and mixing washes. Glass bowls are best, but you can use ceramic or wooden bowls in varying sizes. Have at least two larger bowls, 4-quart (3.8 l) or larger, and two smaller bowls.

Oven mitts: Bread, loaf pans, and the bread machine bucket can be extremely hot, so heat-proof oven mitts, either silicone or cloth, are recommended for handling them.

Parchment paper or silicone mats: Parchment paper or a silicone mat prevents bread from sticking to baking sheets or baking dishes. It also makes cleanup easy—simply wipe the mat or throw away the parchment.

Pastry brush: Brushes can be used for applying egg washes before baking bread and for brushing the finished loaves with melted butter. Look for silicone brushes because they are durable and effortless to clean.

Scale: The recipes in this book do not use a scale to measure the ingredients, but many recipes do use weight. Look for a scale that switches from grams to ounces and can weigh up to at least 4 or 5 pounds (1.8 or 2.27 kg). A scale can also be used to portion dough for loaves or buns and rolls.

Thermometer: Temperature is critical in breadmaking, both the temperature of the ingredients and the baked loaf. Long-stemmed digital instant-read, or probe, thermometers are best.

Wire cooling racks: If you let your baked loaf sit flat on the counter, or in the loaf pan right out of the oven, the steam from the cooling bread can make the loaf soggy. A raised wire cooling rack ensures air circulation under and around the whole loaf so it cools quickly and evenly.

Troubleshooting

Different factors can affect the finished loaves you will bake. A recipe that works beautifully one day might not be successful the next. Sometimes the reason is something as small as the day's humidity or as large as forgetting to add the salt. There is a famous breadmaker who will not bake bread unless it is a sunny day because that is when he is most successful. Whatever the reason, following are a few common issues that can be addressed.

NOT ENOUGH RISE

- Flour has a low gluten content
- Liquid too cold, including adding ingredients from the refrigerator that decrease the temperature
- Liquid too hot and killed the yeast
- Ingredient measurements inaccurate
- Salt in contact with yeast
- Too little yeast
- Too much or too little sugar
- Too much salt
- Stale or inactive yeast
- Kitchen too cold

TOO MUCH RISE

- Too little salt
- Too much yeast

BREAD TOO DENSE

- Underbaked bread
- Inactive yeast
- Oven temperature too hot
- Protein content in flour too low
- Short rising or proofing time
- Too many dried fruits, nuts, vegetables, coconut, or other ingredients
- Too much whole grain, either as additive or flour

CRUST TOO THICK

- Bread doesn't rise high enough
- Dry dough
- Flour has too little gluten, or too much flour used
- Oven temperature too low

STICKY DOUGH

- Flour too low in gluten
- Too much kneading
- Too much liquid, or too little flour

STRANGELY SHAPED BREAD

- Overproofed bread
- Dough not scored
- Oven temperature too low
- Too much yeast

COARSE TEXTURE OR LARGE HOLES

- Dough not kneaded long enough
- Oven temperature too low
- Poorly shaped bread loaves
- Too much flour
- Too much yeast

BREAD COLLAPSES IN OVEN

- Not enough salt
- Too much liquid
- Too much yeast, or wrong type of yeast

PART II

THE RECIPES

So, after reading part 1, you know at least the basic process of breadmaking and how bread machines work. Now, we get to the fun part—the recipes.

About three-quarters of the following recipes use the bread machine to make the dough, and you will form the loaves by hand and bake the bread in a conventional oven.

The remaining recipes are traditional loaves made entirely in the bread machine. All the bread in this book is created with care using quality ingredients—artisan to the last one.

Remember, breadmaking is a science but also needs a little intuition and a generous sprinkling of magic. Recipes can turn out differently every time you put the bread together due to myriad factors, both tangible and intangible. You will learn to read your dough and adjust when required to produce fabulous bread. Above all, enjoy yourself and this incredible activity rooted in tens of thousands of years' creativity and learning. Every time you make a loaf of bread, you are part of this ancient line of bakers.

Chapter Three

TRADITIONAL LOAVES

Butter Whole Wheat Bread

½ cup (120 ml) lukewarm water (100°F to 110°F, or 38°C to 43°C)

½ cup (120 ml) lukewarm milk (100°F to 110°F, or 38°C to 43°C)

3 tablespoons (60 g) maple syrup

¼ cup (60 ml) melted butter, divided

1½ teaspoons sea salt

1¾ cups (210 g) white bread flour, plus more for the work surface

1½ cups (187.5 g) whole wheat flour

2 teaspoons instant dry yeast, or bread machine yeast

Canola oil, for preparing the loaf pan

Yield: 1 loaf

PREP TIME: 10 minutes

RISE TIME: Dough program plus 45 minutes

COOK TIME: 25 minutes

This is the first loaf of bread I made when I started baking at about 10 years old. It is my Nana's recipe to the last smidge of yeast and remains my foolproof loaf for sandwiches and French toast. The original loaf, made more than 40 years ago, was baked in a gorgeous blue-patterned round ceramic loaf pan that since has broken in a move. However, the dough holds up well in a freeform loaf as long as you don't skip the forming steps used to create surface structure. Enjoy!

In the bucket of a bread machine, stir together the water, milk, maple syrup, 3 tablespoons of melted butter, and salt to combine. Add the flours and yeast. Program the machine for Dough and press Start.

Lightly coat a 9 × 5-inch (23 × 13 cm) loaf pan with oil and set aside.

When the cycle is complete, transfer the dough to a lightly floured work surface. Pull one side of the dough up to the center of the ball and gather the opposite side into the center, folding it slightly over the first side. Gather the third side and the fourth until you have a tight package.

Turn the dough over so the gathers are on the bottom. Place both hands on the far side of the ball, cupping it, and gently drag the ball toward you, creating smooth tension on the surface. Rotate the ball a half turn and drag it again to form a smooth log. Place the log in the prepared pan and lightly coat the top of the dough with oil. Cover the pan with plastic wrap and a clean kitchen cloth and set aside to rise until doubled, about 45 minutes.

Preheat the oven to 375°F (190°C).

Bake the bread until golden brown, about 25 minutes. Brush the bread all over with the remaining 1 tablespoon of melted butter and let cool completely. Store in a sealed plastic bag at room temperature for up to 3 days, or freeze in a sealed plastic bag with the air pressed out for up to 2 months (see sidebar on page 23).

Lavender Honey Whole Wheat Bread

1 cup (240 ml) lukewarm water (100°F to 110°F, or 38°C to 43°C)

½ cup (120 ml) lukewarm milk (100°F to 110°F, or 38°C to 43°C)

3 tablespoons (60 g) honey

2 tablespoons (30 ml) canola oil

1 teaspoon salt

2½ cups (312.5 g) whole wheat flour

1½ cups (180 g) white bread flour

2 teaspoons instant dry yeast, or bread machine yeast

Yield: 1 loaf

PREP TIME: 10 minutes

RISE TIME AND COOK TIME: 2-pound (908 g)/Basic program

I have always had a fascination for bees and, as a child, would lie with my face propped up on my palms watching these industrious little insects alight on the flowers in my mother's garden. We had close to four acres of flower gardens, with an entire section devoted to fragrant lavender, and these tall blooms were a favorite of the bees. The honey we purchased from our neighbors held the essence of our lavender, and this subtle flavor infused the bread and cookies baked using this special ingredient.

In the bucket of a bread machine, combine the water, milk, honey, oil, and salt. Add the flours and yeast. Program the machine for Basic, select Light or Medium crust, and press Start.

When the loaf is done, remove the bucket from the machine. Let the loaf cool for 5 minutes, then turn the bucket upside-down and gently shake it to remove the loaf. Transfer to a wire rack to cool completely. Store in a sealed plastic bag at room temperature for up to 3 days, or freeze in a sealed plastic bag with the air pressed out for up to 2 months.

Simple Hearth Bread

1½ cups (360 ml) lukewarm water (100°F to 110°F, or 38°C to 43°C)

2 teaspoons sugar

1½ teaspoons sea salt

3½ cups (420 g) white bread flour, plus more for the work surface

1½ teaspoons instant dry yeast, or bread machine yeast

Canola oil, for preparing the loaf pan

Yield: 1 loaf

PREP TIME: 10 minutes

RISE TIME: Dough program plus 1 hour

COOK TIME: 45 minutes

I whip up a loaf of this crusty bread frequently because the ingredients are staples in my pantry, and probably are in yours, too. You can make this in the bread machine start to finish, but the oven adds a glorious golden crust. In my house, the crust is the favorite part of any baked bread, so I often find "naked" loaves with all the ends and sides cut off. All that remains is the fluffy white center, which is still delicious toasted.

In the bucket of a bread machine, combine the water, sugar, and salt. Add the flour and yeast. Program the machine for Dough and press Start.

Lightly coat a 9 × 5-inch (23 × 13 cm) loaf pan with oil and set aside.

When the cycle is complete, transfer the dough to a lightly floured work surface. Form the dough into a rough 8 ×10-inch (20 × 25 cm) rectangle. Starting from a long edge, tightly roll the dough into a log, pressing the seam to seal it. Place the dough log into the prepared loaf pan. Loosely cover the dough with a clean kitchen cloth and set aside to rise until doubled, about 1 hour.

Preheat the oven to 375°F (190°C).

Bake the bread until golden brown, 40 to 45 minutes. Let the bread cool completely, then store in a sealed plastic bag at room temperature for up to 3 days, or freeze in a sealed plastic bag with the air pressed out for up to 2 months.

Buttermilk Bread

1½ cups (360 ml) lukewarm buttermilk (100°F to 110°F, or 38°C to 43°C)

3 tablespoons (45 ml) melted butter

2 tablespoons (25 g) sugar

1 teaspoon sea salt

3¾ cups (450 g) white bread flour, plus more for the work surface

2¼ teaspoons instant dry yeast, or bread machine yeast

Canola oil, for preparing the loaf pan

Yield: 1 loaf

PREP TIME: 10 minutes

RISE TIME: Dough program plus 45 minutes

COOK TIME: 25 minutes

Buttermilk is a staple baking ingredient in my house for cookies, quick breads, cakes, and, of course, bread. This ingredient adds a wonderful tangy flavor to bread and, when combined with white flour, creates a tender crumb and soft crust. If you do not have buttermilk handy for this recipe, you can create a similar taste and acidity by mixing 1½ cups (360 ml) of milk with 1½ tablespoons (23 ml) of fresh lemon juice or vinegar.

In the bucket of a bread machine, stir together the buttermilk, melted butter, sugar, and salt to combine. Add the flour and yeast. Program the machine for Dough and press Start.

Lightly coat a 9 × 5-inch (23 × 13 cm) loaf pan with oil and set aside.

When the cycle is complete, transfer the dough to a lightly floured work surface. Roll the dough into a rectangle about 8 × 12 inches (20 × 30 cm). Starting from a long end, tightly roll the dough to form a cylinder and place it in the prepared pan. Lightly coat the top of the dough with oil and cover with plastic wrap and a clean kitchen cloth. Set aside until the dough rises about 1½ inches (3.5 cm) above the top of the pan, about 45 minutes.

Using a serrated knife, cut a long slash, about 1 inch (2.5 cm) deep, down the middle of the loaf lengthwise.

Preheat the oven to 350°F (180°C).

Bake the bread until golden brown, about 25 minutes. Let the bread cool completely, then store in a sealed plastic bag at room temperature for up to 3 days, or freeze in a sealed plastic bag with the air pressed out for up to 2 months.

Amish Milk Bread

2 cups (480 ml) lukewarm milk (100°F to 110°F, or 38°C to 43°C)

3 tablespoons (42 g) butter, at room temperature

2 tablespoons (40 g) honey

1 teaspoon sea salt

5½ cups (660 g) white bread flour, plus more for the work surface

1 tablespoon (12 g) instant dry yeast, or bread machine yeast

Canola oil, for preparing the loaf pans and plastic wrap

Yield: 2 loaves

PREP TIME: 10 minutes

RISE TIME: Dough program plus 1 hour

COOK TIME: 45 minutes

I spent almost twenty years living in Waterloo, Ontario, an area famous for its Mennonite communities, and I enjoyed many loaves of a similar tender bread with a generous topping of homemade jam. Although the Amish and Mennonite philosophies are not identical, they share a culinary ideal of quality fresh ingredients and an incredible work ethic. For extra richness, brush the finished loaves with melted butter.

In the bucket of a bread machine, stir together the milk, butter, honey, and salt to combine. Add the flour and yeast. Program the machine for Dough and press Start.

Lightly coat two 9 × 5-inch (23 × 13 cm) loaf pans with oil and set aside.

When the cycle is complete, transfer the dough to a lightly floured work surface. Divide the dough into 2 equal pieces and form each into a log that will fit into the prepared pans. Place the dough in the pans and loosely cover them with lightly oiled plastic wrap. Set the dough aside until doubled, about 1 hour.

Preheat the oven to 350°F (180°C).

Bake the bread until golden brown and the internal temperature reaches 200°F (93°C), 40 to 45 minutes. Let the bread cool completely, then store in a sealed plastic bag at room temperature for up to 3 days, or freeze in a sealed plastic bag with the air pressed out for up to 2 months.

Did you know there is a difference between white Canadian flour and white flour from other parts of the world? The flour recommended in this book is bread flour, but if you are in Canada, you can use all-purpose flour. Canadian all-purpose flour is made with 100 percent hard wheat and consists of 73 percent carbohydrates, 13 percent protein, and 14 percent moisture. All-purpose flour in the United States is 75 percent hard flour and 25 percent soft wheat, so it is not recommended for breadmaking. So, pick up bread flour in the States and the United Kingdom to ensure good results.

Five-Grain Crusty Loaf

1 cup (240 ml) lukewarm water (100°F to 110°F, or 38°C to 43°C)

½ cup (120 ml) lukewarm milk (100°F to 110°F, or 38°C to 43°C)

2 tablespoons (30 ml) canola oil

1 tablespoon (20 g) honey

1½ teaspoons salt

1¾ cups (210 g) white bread flour

1 cup (125 g) whole wheat flour

1 cup (140 g) multigrain cereal

2 teaspoons active dry yeast, or bread machine yeast

Yield: 1 loaf

PREP TIME: 15 minutes

RISE TIME AND COOK TIME:
2-pound (908 g)/Basic program

The best part about baking grain-filled bread is the incredible variety of choices available in the grain category as well as premixed cereals that add five or six types at once. Multigrain cereals can be a more cost-efficient choice if you only use grains occasionally—you won't be buying multiple packages that will sit in your pantry taking up space. If you want to mix your own combination, just make sure the final amount is equal to the cereal amount specified in the recipe. Good choices for this bread include barley, flax, oats, cornmeal, farro, quinoa, wheat berries or cracked wheat, and millet.

In the bucket of a bread machine, combine the water, milk, oil, honey, and salt. Add the flours, cereal, and yeast. Program the machine for Basic, select Medium crust, and press Start.

When the loaf is done, remove the bucket from the machine. Let the loaf cool for 5 minutes, then turn the bucket upside-down and gently shake it to remove the loaf. Transfer to a wire rack to cool completely. Store in a sealed plastic bag at room temperature for up to 3 days, or freeze in a sealed plastic bag with the air pressed out for up to 2 months.

Beer Bread

1 (12-ounce, or 360 ml) bottle lukewarm dark beer (100°F to 110°F, or 38°C to 43°C)

½ cup (120 ml) lukewarm water (100°F to 110°F, or 38°C to 43°C)

1½ teaspoons sea salt

3¾ cups (450 g) white bread flour, plus more for the work surface

1½ teaspoons instant dry yeast, or bread machine yeast

Canola oil, for preparing the baking sheet and the loaf

Yield: 1 loaf

PREP TIME: 10 minutes

RISE TIME: Dough program plus 1 hour

COOK TIME: 30 minutes

Beer bread is often made with no yeast—just beer, sugar, and flour. Some dark beer has visible sediment containing yeast in the bottom of the bottle, so when you add this beer to the dough, it converts the added sugar into the carbon dioxide needed for the bread to rise. This recipe includes extra yeast because the beer you choose might not have enough yeast for a successful loaf.

In the bucket of a bread machine, stir together the beer, water, and salt to combine. Add the flour and yeast. Program the machine for Dough and press Start.

When the cycle is complete, transfer the dough to a lightly floured work surface and pat the dough into a rough ball. Pull one side of the dough up to the center of the ball and gather the opposite side of the ball into the center, folding it slightly over the first side. Then, gather the third side and the fourth side until you have a tight package.

Turn the dough over so the gathers are on the bottom. Place both hands on the far side of the ball, cupping it, and gently drag the ball toward you, creating smooth tension on the surface. Rotate the ball a quarter turn and drag it again. Continue to rotate and drag until the dough is round and the surface is taut.

Coat a baking sheet with oil and place the dough ball on it. Lightly coat the top of the ball with oil. Cover the dough with plastic wrap and a clean kitchen cloth and set aside to rise until doubled, about 1 hour.

Preheat the oven to 450°F (230°C).

Lightly dust the loaf with flour. Cut 3 shallow slashes across the top. Bake until golden brown, 25 to 30 minutes. Let the bread cool completely, then store in a sealed plastic bag at room temperature for up to 3 days, or freeze in a sealed plastic bag with the air pressed out for up to 2 months.

Golden Honey Maple Bread

1¼ cups (300 ml) lukewarm water (100°F to 110°F, or 38°C to 43°C)

2 tablespoons (30 ml) melted butter, cooled

2 tablespoons (40 g) honey

1 tablespoon (20 g) maple syrup

1 teaspoon salt

3½ cups (420 g) white bread flour

2¼ teaspoons instant dry yeast, or bread machine yeast

Yield: 1 loaf

PREP TIME: 10 minutes

RISE TIME AND COOK TIME:
2-pound (908 g)/Basic program

There is a small bakery in my hometown that has been in business for more than 100 years, quietly creating perfect bread that people travel miles to purchase. They sell a loaf that is the absolute ideal sandwich bread—golden crusted, fine crumbed, with a subtle sweetness from two traditional sweeteners. This loaf is an homage to that magnificent creation. If you prefer, make the dough using the Dough setting of a bread machine and do the second rise in a loaf pan for an oven-baked bread. Preheat the oven to 375°F (190°C) and bake for 30 to 35 minutes.

In the bucket of a bread machine, combine the water, melted butter, honey, maple syrup, and salt. Add the flour and yeast. Program the machine for Basic, select Medium crust, and press Start.

When the loaf is done, remove the bucket from the bread machine. Let the loaf cool for 5 minutes, then turn the bucket upside-down and gently shake it to remove the loaf. Transfer to a wired rack to cool completely. Store in a sealed plastic bag at room temperature for up to 3 days, or freeze in a sealed plastic bag with the air pressed out for up to 2 months.

Not all maple syrup is created equally: There are different types of this popular ingredient. In Canada, maple syrup is a national treasure, taken seriously by its producers and consumers alike. Grading is set to international standards and this standard is harmonized across the United States and Canada. The grade is based on grade, color, and taste descriptor. You will have the following choices when purchasing maple syrup for home use:

- Grade A Golden: golden color, delicate taste

- Grade A Amber: slightly darker in color, rich taste

- Grade A Dark: dark color, robust taste

- Grade A Very Dark: very dark color, strong taste

Bran Molasses Bread

1 cup (240 ml) lukewarm water (100°F to 110°F, or 38°C to 43°C)

½ cup (120 ml) lukewarm milk (100°F to 110°F, or 38°C to 43°C)

3 tablespoons (60 g) molasses

2 tablespoons (30 ml) melted butter

2 tablespoons (30 g) packed light brown sugar

1¼ teaspoons salt

1½ cups (180 g) white bread flour

1 cup (125 g) whole wheat flour

1 cup (72 g) whole bran cereal

2 teaspoons instant dry yeast, or bread machine yeast

Yield: 1 loaf

PREP TIME: 10 minutes

RISE TIME AND COOK TIME:
2-pound (908 g)/Basic program

Bran is one of those ingredients people either like or do not like—it has a strong, almost nutty flavor and its texture often requires extra effort to chew. This robust texture is because bran is the hard outer layer of wheat kernels removed during milling and an incredible source of fiber. The best cereal for this bread is not flakes or buds, but the long shreds found in All-Bran Original cereal. It provides a lovely flavor and a hint of structure rather than taking over the whole loaf.

In the bucket of a bread machine, combine the water, milk, molasses, melted butter, brown sugar, and salt. Add the flours, bran cereal, and yeast. Program the machine for Basic, select Medium crust, and press Start.

When the loaf is done, remove the bucket from the bread machine. Let the loaf cool for 5 minutes, then turn the bucket upside-down and gently shake it to remove the loaf. Transfer to a wire rack to cool completely. Store in a sealed plastic bag at room temperature for up to 3 days, or freeze in a sealed plastic bag with the air pressed out for up to 2 months.

Iceland Brown Bread

¾ cup (180 ml) lukewarm water (100°F to 110°F, or 38°C to 43°C)

⅔ cup (160 g) packed light brown sugar

½ cup (120 ml) lukewarm milk (100°F to 110°F, or 38°C to 43°C)

¼ cup (60 ml) melted butter

3 tablespoons (60 g) molasses

2 teaspoons sea salt

3 cups (360 g) white bread flour, plus more for the work surface

1¾ cups (218.75 g) whole wheat flour

2½ teaspoons instant dry yeast, or bread machine yeast

Canola oil, for preparing the loaf pans and plastic wrap

Yield: 2 loaves

PREP TIME: 10 minutes

RISE TIME: Dough program plus 1 hour

COOK TIME: 50 minutes

Brown bread in this context is not the tender whole wheat sandwich bread found in the bakery section of the supermarket; it is a denser loaf made with molasses or coffee to add a darker color and deeper flavor. This bread often has a longer shelf life due to its texture and is fabulous toasted, even when a little stale. You can make this recipe more traditional using 1 cup (125 g) whole wheat flour and ¾ cup (96 g) rye flour.

In the bucket of a bread machine, stir together the water, brown sugar, milk, melted butter, molasses, and salt to combine. Add the flours and yeast. Program the machine for Dough and press Start.

Lightly coat two 9 × 5-inch (23 × 13 cm) loaf pans with oil and set aside.

When the cycle is complete, transfer the dough to a lightly floured work surface. Divide the dough into 2 equal pieces and form each into a rectangle roughly 8 × 10 inches (20 × 25 cm). One at a time, starting from a long edge, roll the dough into a log, pressing the seam to seal it. Place the loaves in the prepared pans. Loosely cover the pans with lightly oiled plastic wrap and a clean kitchen cloth. Set aside until the dough doubles, about 1 hour.

Preheat the oven to 350°F (180°C).

Bake the bread until golden brown and the internal temperature reaches 200°F (93°C), 45 to 50 minutes. Let the bread cool completely, then store in a sealed plastic bag at room temperature for up to 4 days, or freeze in a sealed plastic bag with the air pressed out for up to 2 months.

Russian Black Bread

1¼ cups (300 ml) lukewarm water (100°F to 110°F, or 38°C to 43°C)

2 tablespoons (40 g) blackstrap molasses

2 tablespoons (28 g) butter, at room temperature

2 tablespoons (10 g) unsweetened cocoa powder

1½ tablespoons (23 ml) apple cider vinegar

1 tablespoon (7 g) caraway seeds

1¼ teaspoons sea salt

1 teaspoon espresso powder

1 teaspoon sugar

¼ teaspoon fennel seed

2 cups (256 g) rye flour

1½ cups (180 g) white bread flour, plus more for the work surface

½ cup (36 g) All-Bran cereal

2¼ teaspoons instant dry yeast, or bread machine yeast

Canola oil, for preparing the baking dish and plastic wrap

Yield: 1 loaf

PREP TIME: 10 minutes

RISE TIME: Dough program plus 1 hour, 30 minutes

COOK TIME: 45 minutes

This is not a traditional black bread recipe because it contains some extras; "real" black bread is often just rye flour, a starter, salt, and water. This classic combination produces a very dense loaf with minimal rise, so I like to use yeast and an assortment of flavorings, such as coffee, molasses, fennel seeds, and caraway, to create a lighter finished product. Omit the caraway and fennel if you are not a fan of their subtle licorice taste.

In the bucket of a bread machine, combine the water, molasses, butter, cocoa powder, vinegar, caraway seeds, salt, espresso powder, sugar, and fennel seed. Add the flours and cereal. Make a small well in the top of the ingredients and add the yeast to it. Program the machine for Dough and press Start.

Lightly coat an 8-inch (20 cm) round baking dish with oil and set aside.

When the cycle is complete, remove the dough from the bucket, shape it into a ball, and transfer to a lightly floured work surface. Pull one side of the dough up to the center of the ball and gather the opposite side into the center, folding it slightly over the first side. Gather the third side and the fourth until you have a tight package.

Turn the dough over so the gathers are on the bottom and place both hands on the far side of the ball, cupping it, and gently drag the ball toward you, creating smooth tension on the surface. Rotate the ball a quarter turn and drag it again. Continue to rotate and drag until the dough is round and the surface is taut.

Transfer the ball to the prepared baking dish and cover the dough with lightly oiled plastic wrap. Set aside to rise until doubled, 1 to 1½ hours.

Preheat the oven to 350°F (180°C).

Using a sharp knife, slash an "X" in the top of the loaf. Bake the bread until it sounds hollow when tapped (be careful; it will be hot!) and the internal temperature reaches 205°F (96°C), about 45 minutes. Let the bread cool completely, then store in a sealed plastic bag at room temperature for up to 4 days, or freeze in a sealed plastic bag with the air pressed out for up to 2 months.

Irish Brown Bread

1 cup (240 ml) lukewarm water (100°F to 110°F, or 38°C to 43°C)

½ cup (120 ml) lukewarm buttermilk (100°F to 110°F, or 38°C to 43°C)

2 tablespoons (40 g) blackstrap molasses

1 teaspoon sea salt

2½ cups (312.5 g) whole wheat flour

1½ cups (180 g) white bread flour

2½ teaspoons instant dry yeast, or bread machine yeast

Yield: 1 loaf

PREP TIME: 10 minutes

RISE TIME AND COOK TIME:
2-pound (908 g)/Basic program

I love molasses and specifically look for recipes that use this strong-tasting ingredient. Imagine my delight when I found a recipe in my nana's ingredient-stained cookbook for a family bread recipe featuring molasses. Not just any molasses, but the darkest, blackstrap molasses—a product of the third boil of the syrup left after sugar is removed from the boiled juice of crushed sugar cane or sugar beets. You can use dark molasses, but the bread will lose its intriguing hint of bitterness.

In the bucket of a bread machine, stir together the water, buttermilk, molasses, and salt to combine. Add the flours and yeast. Program the machine for Basic, select Light crust, and press Start.

When the loaf is done, remove the bucket from the machine. Let the loaf cool for 5 minutes, then turn the bucket upside-down and gently shake it to remove the loaf. Transfer to a wire rack to cool completely. Store in a sealed plastic bag at room temperature for up to 3 days, or freeze in a sealed plastic bag with the air pressed out for up to 2 months.

Pretzel Bread

For Dough

¾ cup (180 ml) lukewarm milk (100°F to 110°F, or 38°C to 43°C)

½ cup (120 ml) lukewarm water (100°F to 110°F, or 38°C to 43°C)

2 tablespoons (25 g) sugar

1 tablespoon (15 ml) melted butter

1 teaspoon sea salt

3¼ cups (390 g) white bread flour, plus more for the work surface

2 teaspoons instant dry yeast, or bread machine yeast

Canola oil, for preparing the bowl

For Baking Soda Bath

4 quarts (3.8 l) water

½ cup (110 g) baking soda

For Topping

1 tablespoon (18 g) coarse sea salt

2 tablespoons (30 ml) melted butter (optional)

Yield: 1 loaf

PREP TIME: 10 minutes

RISE TIME: Dough program plus 30 minutes

COOK TIME: 30 minutes

I remember learning that the secret to the texture and taste of pretzels is boiling the dough before baking it. I could not picture exactly how this process would work without the formed loaf flying apart in the water. I was only eight years old, so the intact loaf seemed magical when it emerged unscathed from the simmering pot. When the finished loaf came out of the oven, a rich deep brown with shimmering crystals of coarse salt decorating it, I knew it was magic. Making this bread now still makes me smile.

To make the dough: In the bucket of a bread machine, combine the milk, water, sugar, melted butter, and salt. Add the flour and yeast. Program the machine for Dough and press Start.

When the cycle is complete, transfer the dough to a lightly floured work surface. Pull one side of the dough up to the center of the ball and gather the opposite side into the center, folding it slightly over the first side. Gather the third side and the fourth until you have a tight package.

Turn the dough over so the gathers are on the bottom and place both hands on the far side of the ball, cupping it, and gently drag the ball toward you, creating smooth tension on the surface. Rotate the ball a quarter turn and drag it again. Continue to rotate and drag until the dough is round and the surface is taut.

Lightly coat a medium-size bowl with canola oil and place the dough in it, turning to coat with the oil. Cover the bowl with plastic wrap and a clean kitchen cloth and set aside to rise, about 30 minutes.

Preheat the oven to 400°F (200°C). Line a baking sheet with a silicone baking mat or lightly oiled aluminum foil.

To prepare the baking soda bath: While the dough is rising, bring the water to a boil in a large pot over medium-high heat. Add the baking soda in small quantities until the full amount is used. Do not add it all at once because the mixture will foam up. Place the pretzel bread dough, smooth-side down, into the water and simmer for about 2 minutes. Gently flip it over and simmer for 2 minutes more. Using two slotted spoons, carefully remove the dough from the water and transfer it to the prepared baking sheet.

In Germany, traditional pretzel making included boiling pretzels in a strong lye solution to create the signature deep brown crust. Food-grade lye can be challenging to find and is not the safest ingredient to use in a kitchen, so baking soda is used in many recipes to create the alkaline solution required for the pretzels' signature flavor and color. The alkaline solution enhances the Maillard reaction, a chemical process that causes the browning of foods like bread, but baking soda is not strong enough to create a classic shiny pretzel. Baking the baking soda can strengthen it for the boiling step. Preheat the oven to 250°F (120°C) and spread the baking soda on a baking sheet in a thin layer. Bake for 1 hour. Cool the cooked baking soda, then store in a sealed container at room temperature for up to 1 month.

To make the topping and finish the bread: Using paper towels, pat excess water from the dough. Sprinkle the dough with the coarse salt. Using a sharp knife, slash an "X" in the top.

Bake the bread until dark brown and the internal temperature reaches 190°F (88°C), 20 to 25 minutes. Transfer the baked bread to a wire rack and brush with melted butter if you want a soft crust. Let cool completely before slicing. Store in a sealed plastic bag at room temperature for up to 5 days, or freeze in a sealed plastic bag with the air pressed out for up to 2 months.

Pumpernickel Bread

---

1 cup (240 ml) lukewarm brewed coffee (100°F to 110°F, or 38°C to 43°C)

¼ cup (80 g) dark molasses

3 tablespoons (45 ml) melted butter, cooled

2 tablespoons (10 g) unsweetened cocoa powder

1 tablespoon (12.5 g) granulated sugar

1½ teaspoons salt

2 cups (256 g) dark rye flour

2 cups (250 g) whole wheat bread flour, plus more as needed and for the work surface

2 teaspoons caraway seeds (optional)

2¼ teaspoons instant dry yeast, or bread machine yeast

Canola oil, for preparing the bowl and baking dish

Yield: 1 loaf

PREP TIME: 10 minutes

RISE TIME: Dough program plus 2 hours

COOK TIME: 40 minutes

I always wondered about the secret ingredient in the dark, fragrant bread my Dutch mother served us for lunch with an assortment of meats, Gouda cheese, and thinly sliced cucumber. When I started baking round loaves of pumpernickel as a chef, I found out the secret is my favorite things in the whole world—coffee and chocolate. Well, unsweetened cocoa powder, but close enough! This loaf sometimes takes a little extra time to rise and the resulting bread is quite dense and rustic, but utterly delicious.

In the bucket of a bread machine, combine the coffee, molasses, melted butter, cocoa powder, sugar, and salt. Add the flours, caraway seeds (if using), and yeast. Program the machine for Dough and press Start.

After 15 minutes of the kneading cycle, check the dough to see if it is tacky and soft. If it is too dry, add water, 1 teaspoon at a time. If the dough is too wet, add whole wheat flour 1 tablespoon at a time.

When the cycle is complete, gather the dough into a ball and transfer it to a large oiled bowl, turning to coat the top in oil. Cover the bowl with a clean kitchen cloth and let rise for 1 to 1½ hours.

Lightly coat an 8-inch (20 cm) round baking pan with oil and set aside.

Turn the dough out onto a lightly floured work surface and shape it into a round loaf, using your hands to tuck the bottom edges under the ball tightly. Transfer the dough to the prepared baking pan, cover with a clean kitchen cloth, and let rise for 30 minutes more.

Preheat the oven to 400°F (200°C).

Bake the bread until it sounds hollow when tapped (be careful; it will be hot!) and the internal temperature reaches 210°F (99°C), 35 to 40 minutes. Transfer the bread to a wire rack to cool completely. Store in a sealed plastic bag at room temperature for up to 3 days, or freeze in a sealed plastic bag with the air pressed out for up to 2 months.

When Napoleon was conducting his Prussian campaign, he demanded a loaf of bread for his horse, Nicole, in his native French. "*Pain pour Nicole*" sounded to the local Germans like "pumpernickel," which is what this bread is called now.

Rustic German Rye

2 cups (480 ml) lukewarm water (100°F to 110°F, or 38°C to 43°C)

½ cup (160 g) molasses

¼ cup (60 ml) melted butter

¼ cup (20 g) unsweetened cocoa powder

1 tablespoon (7 g) caraway seeds

2½ teaspoons sea salt

3 cups (384 g) rye flour

2½ cups (300 g) white bread flour, plus more for the work surface

2¼ teaspoons instant dry yeast, or bread machine yeast

Canola oil, for preparing the baking sheet and loaves

Yield: 2 loaves

PREP TIME: 15 minutes

RISE TIME: Dough program plus 1 hour

COOK TIME: 30 minutes

Rye bread was a staple of my childhood lunches because it is firm and has such a glorious earthy taste. My Dutch mother would set up baskets of meats, cheeses, jams, chocolate spread, and sugar sprinkles alongside rye bread, rusks, and baguette slices to create the fixings for open-face sandwiches. *Broodjes* are still my favorite lunch, although I skip the chocolate and sugar toppings now.

In the bucket of a bread machine, combine the water, molasses, melted butter, cocoa powder, caraway seeds, and salt. Add the flours and yeast. Program the machine for Dough and press Start.

When the cycle is complete, transfer the dough to a lightly floured work surface and divide the dough into 2 equal pieces. Working with 1 piece at a time, pull one side of the dough up to the center of the ball and gather the opposite side into the center, folding it slightly over the first side. Gather the third side and the fourth until you have a tight package.

Turn the dough over so the gathers are on the bottom and place both hands on the far side of the ball, cupping it, and gently drag the ball toward you, creating smooth tension on the surface. Rotate the ball a quarter turn and drag it again. Continue to rotate and drag until the dough is round and the surface is taut. Repeat with the second dough.

Lightly coat a baking sheet with oil. Place the loaves on it and lightly coat them with oil, loosely cover them with plastic wrap, and let rise for 1 hour.

Preheat the oven to 400°F (200°C).

Using a serrated knife, cut 2 diagonal slashes in the top of each loaf about 1 inch (2.5 cm) deep. Bake the loaves until deep brown and the internal temperature reaches 210°F (99°C), about 30 minutes.

Let the bread cool for at least 1 hour before cutting it. Refrigerate leftovers in a sealed plastic bag for up to 4 days, or freeze in a sealed plastic bag with the air pressed out for up to 2 months.

Because rye flour contains a different gluten-forming protein than white flour or whole wheat flour, rye bread can be very dense. If you want lighter rye bread, cut the rye flour with white flour, or add vital wheat gluten to the dough. Rye bread can take more time to rise as well, so be patient.

Traditional Rye Bread

1¼ cups (300 ml) lukewarm water (100°F to 110°F, or 38°C to 43°C)

¼ cup (80 g) molasses

2 tablespoons (30 ml) canola oil, plus more for preparing the loaf pan

1 teaspoon salt

2 cups (240 g) white bread flour, plus more for the work surface

1½ cups (192 g) rye flour

3 tablespoons (10 g) dry potato flakes

2½ teaspoons instant dry yeast, or bread machine yeast

Yield: 1 loaf

PREP TIME: 10 minutes

RISE TIME: Dough program plus 1 hour

COOK TIME: 30 minutes

When offered a choice of white, brown, or rye bread in restaurants, I always chose rye. Part of my heritage is Scandinavian and the firm, slightly sour bread is perfect for hearty corned beef sandwiches, toast topped with peanut butter, and eaten plain with a little smear of butter as a snack. This is basic rye with added richness from potato flakes. If you want to jazz it up, throw in 1 tablespoon (7 g) caraway seeds or ½ cup (36 g) sunflower seeds with the flours.

In the bucket of a bread machine, combine the water, molasses, oil, and salt. Add the flours, potato flakes, and yeast. Program the machine for Dough and press Start.

Lightly coat a 9 × 5-inch (23 × 13 cm) loaf pan with oil and set aside.

When the cycle is complete, turn the dough out onto a lightly floured work surface. Shape the dough into a log, using your hands to tuck the edges under the dough ball to create a smooth top. Place the dough into the prepared loaf pan, cover with a clean kitchen cloth, and let rise until doubled, about 1 hour.

Preheat the oven to 375°F (190°C).

Bake the bread until golden brown and the internal temperature reaches 190°F (88°C), 25 to 30 minutes. If the loaf browns too quickly, loosely cover the top with aluminum foil. Let the bread cool for 5 minutes, then remove it from the loaf pan and let cool completely. Store in a sealed plastic bag at room temperature for up to 3 days, or freeze in a sealed plastic bag with the air pressed out for up to 2 months.

Potato flakes might seem like a strange ingredient in bread, but this ingredient creates a moist, fluffy, tender loaf. Potato flakes will also keep the finished bread fresher longer.

Swedish Rye

1¼ cups (300 ml) lukewarm water (100°F to 110°F, or 38°C to 43°C)

3 tablespoons (45 g) packed light brown sugar

3 tablespoons (60 g) dark molasses

3 tablespoons (45 ml) melted butter, divided

Grated zest of ½ orange

1 teaspoon sea salt

½ teaspoon aniseed

2 cups (240 g) white bread flour, plus more for the work surface

2 cups (256 g) rye flour

2¼ teaspoons instant dry yeast, or bread machine yeast

Canola oil, for preparing the baking sheet

1 tablespoon (9 g) cornmeal

Yield: 1 loaf

PREP TIME: 10 minutes

RISE TIME: Dough program plus 45 minutes

COOK TIME: 30 minutes

This loaf is inspired by Swedish limpa bread, with hints of orange, licorice, and molasses. This is the ideal bread for any type of sandwich—from scoops of tuna salad to grilled vegetables and tangy goat cheese. The dense crumb ensures the toppings won't leak out and the bread will hold together until the last bite.

In the bucket of a bread machine, combine the water, brown sugar, molasses, 2 tablespoons of melted butter, orange zest, salt, and aniseed. Add the flours and yeast. Program the machine for Dough and press Start.

Lightly coat a baking sheet with oil, sprinkle it with cornmeal, and set aside.

When the cycle is complete, turn the dough out onto a lightly floured work surface and punch it down. Shape the dough into an oval loaf. Using your hands in a cupping motion, rotate the dough, tucking the sides under to create a smooth, taut surface. Place the loaf on the prepared baking sheet and loosely cover it with a clean kitchen cloth. Set aside to double, about 45 minutes.

Preheat the oven to 350°F (180°C).

Using a serrated knife, cut 4 or 5 shallow diagonal slashes on the top of the loaf. Bake until golden, about 30 minutes. Transfer the loaf to a wire rack and brush it with the remaining 1 tablespoon of melted butter. Let the bread cool completely, then store in a sealed plastic bag at room temperature for up to 3 days, or freeze in a sealed plastic bag with the air pressed out for up to 2 months.

Oatmeal Kefir Bread

1 cup (240 ml) lukewarm water (100°F to 110°F, or 38°C to 43°C)

½ cup (120 ml) lukewarm kefir (100°F to 110°F, or 38°C to 43°C)

3 tablespoons (45 ml) melted butter

3 tablespoons (45 g) packed dark brown sugar

1¼ teaspoons sea salt

3½ cups (420 g) white bread flour, plus more for the work surface

1 cup (156 g) rolled oats

2 teaspoons instant dry yeast, or bread machine yeast

Canola oil, for preparing the loaf pan

Yield: 1 loaf

PREP TIME: 10 minutes

RISE TIME: Dough program plus 30 minutes

COOK TIME: 35 minutes

Kefir is a fermented beverage with a taste similar to tangy yogurt. It is made with a starter similar to sourdough bread and can be found in dairy and nondairy varieties. Kefir adds flavor, a tender texture, and many nutrients to this slightly sweet loaf. You can make this entirely in the bread machine instead of baking it; just program 2 pound (908 g)/ Basic, Medium crust, and Start. Soon you will be enjoying a slice of oatmeal-packed bread with your favorite toppings or a simple smear of butter.

In the bucket of a bread machine, combine the water, kefir, melted butter, brown sugar, and salt. Add the flour, oats, and yeast. Program the machine for Dough and press Start.

Lightly coat a 9 × 5-inch (23 × 13 cm) loaf pan with oil and set aside.

When the cycle is complete, transfer the dough to a lightly floured work surface. Pull one side of the dough up to the center of the ball and gather the opposite side into the center, folding it slightly over the first side. Gather the third side and the fourth until you have a tight package.

Turn the dough over so the gathers are on the bottom, place your hands on each side of the ball, and pull the dough under on both sides, creating a log for a loaf pan. Transfer the smooth dough log to the prepared pan. Lightly coat the top of the dough with oil and cover it with plastic wrap and a clean kitchen cloth. Set aside until doubled, about 30 minutes.

Preheat the oven to 350°F (180°C).

Bake the bread until golden brown and the internal temperature reaches 190°F (88°C), about 35 minutes. Let the bread cool completely, then store in a sealed plastic bag at room temperature for up to 5 days, or freeze in a sealed plastic bag with the air pressed out for up to 2 months.

Spelt Bread

- - - - - - - - - - - - - - - - - - - -

⅔ cup (160 ml) lukewarm water (100°F to 110°F, or 38°C to 43°C)

⅔ cup (160 ml) lukewarm milk (100°F to 110°F, or 38°C to 43°C)

3 tablespoons (60 g) molasses

1½ tablespoons (23 ml) melted butter

1¼ teaspoons salt

2½ cups (300 g) white bread flour

1¾ cups (173.25 g) spelt flour

2 teaspoons instant dry yeast, or bread machine yeast

Yield: 1 loaf

PREP TIME: 10 minutes

RISE TIME AND COOK TIME: 2-pound (908 g)/Basic program

Spelt is an ancient grain, sometimes thought to be the "parent" of wheat used in almost everything today. Spelt is not gluten free, but it is sometimes tolerated by people with this sensitivity because the gluten it contains is more water soluble and digestible than standard wheat. Bread baked with spelt is tender and light with a pleasant, almost sweet, nutty flavor.

In the bucket of a bread machine, stir together the water, milk, molasses, melted butter, and salt to combine. Add the flours and yeast. Program the machine for Basic, select Light or Medium crust, and press Start.

When the loaf is done, remove the bucket from the machine. Let the loaf cool for 5 minutes, then turn the bucket upside-down and gently shake it to remove the loaf. Transfer to a wire rack to cool completely. Store in a sealed plastic bag at room temperature for up to 3 days, or freeze in a sealed plastic bag with the air pressed out for up to 2 months.

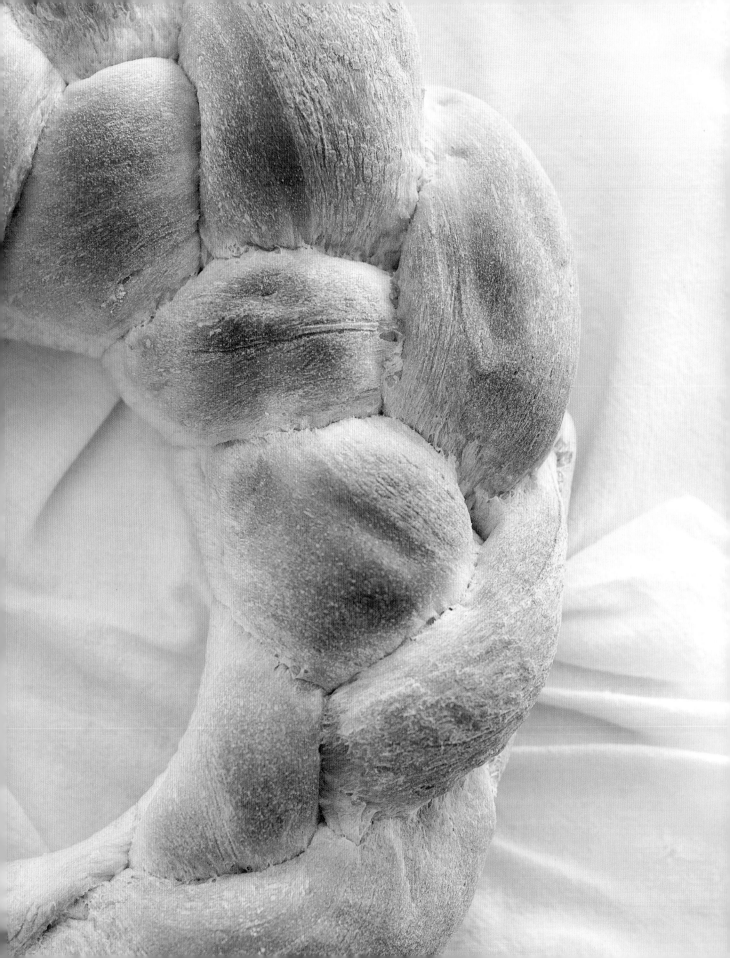

Chapter Four

CLASSIC CRUSTY LOAVES

Baguette

For Starter

1 cup (120 g) white bread flour

½ cup (120 ml) lukewarm water (100°F to 110°F, or 38°C to 43°C)

¼ teaspoon active dry yeast

For Dough

1 cup (120 ml) lukewarm water (100°F to 110°F, or 38°C to 43°C)

2¼ teaspoons sea salt

3½ cups (420 g) white bread flour, plus more for the work surface

1¾ teaspoons instant dry yeast, or bread machine yeast

Canola oil, for preparing the baking sheet

Yield: 3 loaves

PREP TIME: 20 minutes

RISE TIME: Dough program plus 2 hours, 15 minutes, plus 24 hours for the starter

COOK TIME: 28 minutes

Do not let the length of this recipe scare you; the results are worth it. Baking perfect baguettes is a culinary triumph that seasoned chefs work to achieve. The trick to creating the signature baguette shape is in the folding, pressing the dough hard to seal it together and creating the overlapping dough that opens up when baked. If the dough shrinks too much when you are rolling it into cylinders, let it rest for a few minutes to let the gluten relax and try again.

To make the starter: In a medium bowl, stir together the flour, water, and yeast until well combined. Tightly cover the bowl with plastic wrap. Set aside at room temperature for 18 to 24 hours until bubbly and doubled in size.

To make the dough: Scrape the starter into the bucket of a bread machine and add the water and salt. Add the flour and yeast. Program the machine for Dough and press Start.

When the cycle is complete, transfer the dough to a lightly oiled medium-size bowl, tucking the sides under to form a tight ball. Cover the bowl with plastic wrap and let the dough rise for 1 hour.

Turn the dough out onto a lightly floured work surface and cut the dough into 3 equal pieces. Form each piece into a ball, tucking the bottom edges under. Cover the balls with plastic wrap and let rest for 15 to 30 minutes to relax the gluten.

Lightly coat a baking sheet with oil and set aside.

Working with 1 piece at a time, flatten the dough into a rectangle about ½ inch (1 cm) thick. Position the rectangle so the long sides are parallel to you and the work surface edge. Fold the top of the dough over to the middle of the rectangle and use your fingers to seal the seam. Fold the bottom edge of the dough over to the center, sealing the seam right up against the top edge. Press your fingertips into the dough to make the center indentation deeper.

Fold the top edge over about one-third of the way, using your left hand while pressing the heel of your right on the edge of the fold, sealing it. Repeat with a second fold from the bottom, over the first to the center indentation, pressing with the heel of your right hand again to seal.

If you are having an issue with your bread rising, and are doing everything as directed, it could be your water. Municipal water supplies are often heavily chlorinated or treated for health reasons, which can affect the rise. Try filtered or bottled water if in doubt about your water.

Now, fold the dough entirely in half so the bottom edge and top edge are lined up, sealing the dough completely to form a relatively smooth cylinder.

With seam-side down, start in the middle of the dough and, using both hands, moving outward, gently roll the dough, pressing slightly toward the outsides to elongate the baguette. Repeat this rolling technique until you have a 16-inch (40.5 cm)-long baguette with tapered ends. Place the baguette on the prepared baking sheet.

Repeat with the remaining dough.

Cover the baguettes with plastic wrap and set aside to rise slightly, not quite double, about 45 minutes.

Preheat the oven to 450°F (230°C) and place a large baking dish on the bottom oven rack.

Using a knife, cut 4 diagonal slashes in the baguettes and place them in the oven. Pour about 2 cups (480 ml) of boiling water in the baking dish and close the door. Bake the baguettes until deep golden brown, 25 to 28 minutes. Let the bread cool completely, then store in a sealed plastic bag at room temperature for 1 day, or freeze in a sealed plastic bag with the air pressed out for up to 2 months.

Whole Wheat Baguettes

1¾ cups (420 ml) lukewarm water (100°F to 110°F, or 38°C to 43°C)

2 tablespoons (30 g) packed light brown sugar

3 tablespoons (45 ml) olive oil, divided, plus more for the plastic wrap

2 teaspoons sea salt

2½ cups (312.5 g) whole wheat flour

1¼ cups (150 g) white bread flour, plus more for the work surface

¼ cup (38 g) flaxseed

2¼ teaspoons instant dry yeast, or bread machine yeast

Cornmeal, for dusting

Rolled oats, for topping

Yield: 2 loaves

PREP TIME: 30 minutes

RISE TIME: Dough program plus 1 hour, 15 minutes

COOK TIME: 20 minutes

Whole wheat is my personal preference for bread, along with rye, multigrain, or anything that adds texture and taste. The addition of whole wheat flour creates baguettes with a softer crust than standard white loaves. This softness means you can enjoy the whole wheat loaves for several days without the exterior getting too hard to bite into comfortably.

In the bucket of a bread machine, combine the water, brown sugar, 2 tablespoons (30 ml) of oil, and salt. Add the flours, flaxseed, and yeast. Program the machine for Dough and press Start.

When the cycle is complete, transfer the dough to a lightly floured work surface. Cut the dough into 2 equal pieces and form each piece into a ball, tucking the bottom edges under.

Cover the balls with plastic wrap and let rest for 15 to 30 minutes to relax the gluten.

Line a baking sheet with parchment paper and dust with cornmeal.

Working with one piece of dough at a time, flatten the dough into a rectangle about 6 × 12 inches (15 × 30 cm). Starting from a long side, tightly roll the rectangle to create a long, narrow loaf. Seal the seam and ends, tapering the ends slightly. Place the loaf on the prepared baking sheet and repeat with the remaining dough.

Using a serrated knife, cut 4 diagonal slashes in each loaf, cover with lightly oiled plastic wrap, and set aside to rise slightly, not quite doubled, about 45 minutes.

Preheat the oven to 400°F (200°C).

Brush the loaves with the remaining 1 tablespoon (15 ml) of oil and sprinkle with oats.

Bake the baguettes until golden brown and crisp, 15 to 20 minutes. Let the bread cool completely, then store in a sealed plastic bag at room temperature for 1 day, or freeze in a sealed plastic bag with the air pressed out for up to 2 months.

Batarde

1½ cups (360 ml) lukewarm water (100°F to 110°F, or 38°C to 43°C)

1 tablespoon (12.5 g) sugar

2 teaspoons sea salt

4 cups (480 g) white bread flour, plus more for the work surface and the loaves

2¼ teaspoons instant dry yeast, or bread machine yeast

Yield: 2 loaves

PREP TIME: 30 minutes

RISE TIME: Dough program plus 30 minutes

COOK TIME: 30 minutes

Batarde bread is very similar to baguettes but shorter and wider. The technique for creating these crusty loaves is not as intricate as classic baguettes, so this recipe can be a good starting point in French bread baking. The slightly flatter batarde loaf slices beautifully lengthwise for delicious sandwiches with the perfect ratio of bread to filling.

In the bucket of a bread machine, combine the water, sugar, and salt. Add the flour and yeast. Program the machine for Dough and press Start.

When the cycle is complete, turn the dough out onto a lightly floured work surface. Divide the dough into 2 equal pieces and set one aside under a clean kitchen cloth.

Line a baking sheet with parchment paper and set aside.

Stretch and pat the other piece into a thick circle about 10 inches (25 cm) in diameter. Fold the left side of the circle over the middle to overlap the other side by about 1 inch (2.5 cm). Fold the right side over the middle to overlap the other fold by about 1 inch (2.5 cm). Fold the top over the middle, overlapping the middle by about 1 inch (2.5 cm), gently pressing to seal the dough without removing too much air. Fold the top of the dough over once more, rolling it toward you, sealing the edge with your fingers. Continue to roll and seal, creating a smooth, taut surface in the shape of a thick log. Place the loaf on the prepared baking sheet and repeat with the remaining dough.

Dust the tops of the loaves with flour and cover them with a clean kitchen cloth. Set aside to rise until doubled, about 30 minutes.

Preheat the oven to 400°F (200°C).

Using a serrated knife, cut 4 small diagonal slashes in the tops of the loaves. Spritz the dough with cold water and bake until golden brown, about 30 minutes. Let the bread cool completely, then store in a sealed plastic bag at room temperature for up to 2 days, or freeze in a sealed plastic bag with the air pressed out for up to 2 months.

Pain de Campagne

For Starter

1 cup (240 ml) lukewarm water (100°F to 110°F, or 38°C to 43°C)

1 cup (120 g) white bread flour

½ cup (62.5 g) whole wheat flour

½ teaspoon dry active yeast

For Dough

1 cup (240 ml) lukewarm water (100°F to 110°F, or 38°C to 43°C)

1½ tablespoons (18.75 g) sugar

1½ teaspoons sea salt

3¼ cups (390 g) white bread flour, plus more for the work surface

½ cup (64 g) rye flour

1 teaspoon active dry yeast

Canola oil, for preparing the baking dish and plastic wrap

Yield: 1 loaf

PREP TIME: 20 minutes

RISE TIME: Dough program plus 1 hour, 30 minutes, plus 12 hours for the starter

COOK TIME: 30 minutes

The signature sour taste of *pain de campagne*, or French sourdough, is thanks to letting the starter sit, so don't rush that process. You can also deepen the flavor by letting the finished dough ferment in a bowl covered with plastic wrap in the refrigerator. Watch the dough and punch it down if it rises too much. After three to four hours, take the dough out and continue with the recipe as written.

To make the starter: In a medium bowl, stir together the water, flours, and yeast until well combined. Tightly cover the bowl with plastic wrap. Set aside at room temperature for 10 to 12 hours until bubbly. The longer it sits, the better the taste of the finished bread.

To make the dough: Scrape the starter into the bucket of a bread machine and add the water, sugar, and salt. Add the flour and yeast. Program the machine for Dough and press Start.

Lightly coat a 9-inch (23 cm) round baking dish with oil and set aside.

When the cycle is complete, remove the dough from the bucket, shape it into a ball, and transfer to a lightly floured work surface. Pull one side of the dough up to the center of the ball and gather the opposite side into the center, folding it slightly over the first side. Gather the third side and the fourth until you have a tight package.

Turn the dough over so the gathers are on the bottom and place both hands on the far side of the ball, cupping it, and gently drag the ball toward you, creating smooth tension on the surface. Rotate the ball a quarter turn and drag it again. Continue to rotate and drag until the dough is round and the surface is taut. Transfer the ball to the prepared baking dish, cover with lightly oiled plastic wrap, and set aside to rise until doubled, 1 to 1½ hours.

Preheat the oven to 450°F (230°C) and place a pan on the lower rack.

Using a sharp knife, slash a square on the top of the loaf, or cut 3 diagonal slashes. Place the bread in the oven. Add 5 or 6 ice cubes to the pan on the lower rack.

Bake the loaf until golden brown and the internal temperature reaches 190°F (88°C), 25 to 30 minutes. Let the bread cool completely, then store in a sealed plastic bag at room temperature for up to 2 days, or freeze in a sealed plastic bag with the air pressed out for up to 2 months.

Honey French Bread

1 cup (240 ml) lukewarm water (100°F to 110°F, or 38°C to 43°C)

3 tablespoons (60 g) honey

1¼ teaspoons sea salt

3 cups (360 g) white bread flour, plus more for the work surface

1½ teaspoons instant dry yeast, or bread machine yeast

Yield: 1 loaf

PREP TIME: 15 minutes

RISE TIME: Dough program plus 55 minutes

COOK TIME: 20 minutes

When you purchase a loaf of French bread in the supermarket, it is probably very similar to this thin-crusted creation. The honey adds an appetizing sweetness and helps brown the crust. Try using thick slices of honey French bread to make a sliced chicken, Gouda, and red pepper jelly sandwich for a filling lunch or dinner. Delicious!

In the bucket of a bread machine, combine the water, honey, and salt. Add the flour and yeast. Program the machine for Dough and press Start.

When the cycle is complete, turn the dough out onto a lightly floured work surface and let it rest for 10 minutes.

Line a baking sheet with parchment paper and set aside.

Roll the dough into a rectangle about 1 inch (2.5 cm) thick and 12 inches (30 cm) on the long side. Starting from the long side, tightly roll the dough into a cylinder. Pinch the edges to seal and tuck under the ends to create a smooth finish. Place the cylinder on the prepared baking sheet and cover with a clean kitchen cloth. Set aside to rise for about 45 minutes.

Preheat the oven to 400°F (200°C).

Using a serrated knife, cut 4 or 5 diagonal slashes on the top of the loaf. Bake until golden, about 20 minutes. Let the bread cool completely, then store in a sealed plastic bag at room temperature for up to 3 days, or freeze in a sealed plastic bag with the air pressed out for up to 2 months.

Adding vital wheat gluten to the dry ingredients can increase the rise of your bread, making it light and airy. If using this ingredient, add about 1 tablespoon (7.5 g) per cup of bread for a good result.

Golden Oat Bran Bread

1 cup (240 ml) lukewarm water (100°F to 110°F, or 38°C to 43°C)

1 cup (240 ml) lukewarm milk (100°F to 110°F, or 38°C to 43°C)

2 tablespoons (30 ml) melted butter

2 tablespoons (40 g) honey

1¾ teaspoons sea salt

2 cups (250 g) whole wheat flour

2 cups (240 g) white bread flour

1 cup (100 g) oat bran

2¼ teaspoons instant dry yeast, or bread machine yeast

Yield: 1 loaf

PREP TIME: 10 minutes

RISE TIME AND COOK TIME:
2-pound (908 g)/Basic program

Oat bran is not just an ingredient for healthy muffins or fiber-packed smoothies; it can contribute to a flavorsome bread as well. Oat bran is the outer layer of the oat grain, removed during the milling process, so it contains the nutritional benefits of oats, such as high fiber and many vitamins and minerals. Oat bran is not strongly flavored but combines well with the other ingredients in this recipe to create a denser loaf.

In the bucket of a bread machine, stir together the water, milk, melted butter, honey, and salt to combine. Add the flours, oat bran, and yeast. Program the machine for Basic, select Light crust, and press Start.

When the loaf is done, remove the bucket from the machine. Let the loaf cool for 5 minutes, then turn the bucket upside-down and gently shake it to remove the loaf. Transfer to a wire rack to cool completely. Store in a sealed plastic bag at room temperature for up to 3 days, or freeze in a sealed plastic bag with the air pressed out for up to 2 months.

Sesame French Bread Swirl

¾ cup (180 ml) lukewarm water (100°F to 110°F, or 38°C to 43°C)

½ cup (120 ml) lukewarm milk (100°F to 110°F, or 38°C to 43°C)

1 tablespoon (15 g) packed light brown sugar

1 tablespoon (15 ml) melted butter

1½ teaspoons sea salt

3¼ cups (390 g) white bread flour, plus more for the work surface

2¼ teaspoons instant dry yeast, or bread machine yeast

Canola oil, for preparing the plastic wrap

1 large egg white

1 tablespoon (15 ml) water

3 tablespoons (24 g) sesame seeds (see sidebar on page 35)

Yield: 2 loaves

PREP TIME: 20 minutes

RISE TIME: Dough program plus 1 hour

COOK TIME: 25 minutes

The unusual "S" shape of these loaves looks spectacular on a cutting board set on a table for special guests. The rich sesame flavor and tender, slightly sweet interior of this bread can pair with almost any meal—from casseroles to grilled meats to a simple salad. When you cut the spiral design, the bread is one solid piece, so it can be toasted and slathered with butter for a real treat.

In the bucket of a bread machine, combine the lukewarm water, milk, brown sugar, melted butter, and salt. Add the flour and yeast. Program the machine for Dough and press Start.

Line a baking sheet with parchment paper and set aside.

When the cycle is complete, turn the dough out onto a lightly floured work surface and punch it down. Divide the dough into 2 equal pieces. Roll each piece into a 16-inch (40.5 cm) rope and stretch one out straight, marking the center of the rope.

Starting at one end, coil the rope to the center, then starting at the other end, coil that end to the center on the opposite side, creating an "S" shape. Place the loaf on the prepared baking sheet and repeat with the remaining rope.

Cover the loaves with lightly oiled plastic wrap and set aside until doubled, about 1 hour.

Preheat the oven to 350°F (180°C).

In a small bowl, whisk the egg white and water. Brush the egg wash on the loaves and generously sprinkle with sesame seeds.

Bake the loaves until golden brown, about 25 minutes. Let the bread cool completely, then store in a sealed plastic bag at room temperature for up to 4 days, or freeze in a sealed plastic bag with the air pressed out for up to 2 months.

Ciabatta

For Starter
1¼ cups (150 g) white bread flour

1 cup (240 ml) lukewarm water (100°F to 110°F, or 38°C to 43°C)

½ teaspoon active dry yeast

For Dough
1 cup (240 ml) lukewarm water (100°F to 110°F, or 38°C to 43°C)

3 cups (360 g) white bread flour, plus more for the work surface and the dough

½ teaspoon sea salt

Yield: 2 loaves

PREP TIME: 15 minutes

RISE TIME: Dough program plus 40 minutes, plus 24 hours for the starter

COOK TIME: 25 minutes

My husband has a love affair with Italian bread due to his time spent playing professional hockey in that country. He looks for ciabatta bread in every bakery and it is his number-one choice for any sandwich or accompaniment to meals. The porous texture and chewy, but still crisp, crust is exceptional. When I first made this recipe for him, he nearly proposed all over again.

To make the starter: In a medium bowl, stir together the flour, water, and yeast until you have a smooth mixture. Cover the bowl with plastic wrap and refrigerate for between 12 and 24 hours—the longer, the better for the finished bread.

To make the dough: Scrape the starter into the bucket of a bread machine and stir in the water. Add the flour and salt. Program the machine for Dough and press Start.

When the cycle is complete, scrape the dough onto a well-floured work surface; the dough will be sticky. Do not handle the dough too much or you will knock the air out of it. Sprinkle the dough with flour and use a scraper to form the dough into a rough 8 × 8-inch (20 × 20 cm) square. Cut the dough down the middle to create two 4 × 8-inch (10 × 20 cm) loaves. Gently move them apart to preserve the air. Flour the top of the loaves and place a clean kitchen towel over them. Let rise until very puffy, 35 to 40 minutes.

Place an oven rack in the lowest position and preheat the oven to 475°F (240°C). Line a baking sheet with parchment paper and set aside.

Using your hands, carefully transfer the risen loaves to the prepared baking sheet. Dust off any excess flour from the top and lightly spray the loaves with water.

Bake the bread until golden brown and the internal temperature reaches 205°F (96°C), about 25 minutes. Transfer the bread to a wire rack to cool completely. Store in a sealed plastic bag at room temperature for 1 day, or freeze in a sealed plastic bag with the air pressed out for up to 2 months.

Pagnotta

1½ cups (360 ml) lukewarm water (100°F to 110°F, or 38°C to 43°C)

1 tablespoon (15 ml) olive oil

1 tablespoon (15 g) packed light brown sugar

1¼ teaspoons sea salt

3½ cups (420 g) white bread flour, plus more for the work surface and the loaf

1½ teaspoons instant dry yeast, or bread machine yeast

Yield: 1 loaf

PREP TIME: 15 minutes

RISE TIME: Dough program plus 45 minutes

COOK TIME: 30 minutes

Italian bread is renowned for its crusts and is often used when a recipe requires a hollowed-out loaf as a bowl for stew or soup because the bread holds its shape. Pagnotta has this thick golden crust along with an unexpectedly soft interior. Traditional versions can utilize a starter, but this recipe without the starter produces a lovely bread to enjoy in less time.

In the bucket of a bread machine, combine the water, oil, brown sugar, and salt. Add the flour and yeast. Program the machine for Dough and press Start.

When the cycle is complete, remove the dough from the bucket, shape it into a ball, and transfer to a lightly floured work surface. Pull one side of the dough up to the center of the ball and gather the opposite side into the center, folding it slightly over the first side. Gather the third side and the fourth until you have a tight package.

Turn the dough over so the gathers are on the bottom and place both hands on the far side of the ball, cupping it, and gently drag the ball toward you, creating smooth tension on the surface. Rotate the ball a quarter turn and drag it again. Continue to rotate and drag until the dough is round and the surface is taut. Transfer the ball, seam-side up, to the medium-size bowl lined with a clean kitchen towel and dusted with flour. Cover the bowl with another cloth and set aside until doubled, about 45 minutes.

Preheat the oven to 400°F (200°C). Place an ovenproof baking dish on the bottom oven rack. Line a baking sheet with parchment paper and tip the loaf out onto it, seam-side down. Add 2 or 3 ice cubes to the pan on the lower rack to create steam.

Bake the bread until golden brown and the internal temperature reaches 190°F (88°), about 30 minutes. Let the bread cool completely, then store in a sealed plastic bag at room temperature for up to 6 days, or freeze in a sealed plastic bag with the air pressed out for up to 2 months.

Tuscan Bread

For Starter
¾ cup (90 g) white bread flour

¼ cup (60 ml) lukewarm water (100°F to 110°F, or 38°C to 43°C)

¼ teaspoon active dry yeast

For Dough
1¼ cups (300 ml) lukewarm water (100°F to 110°F, or 38°C to 43°C)

3¼ cups (390 g) white bread flour, plus more for the work surface

Cornmeal, for dusting

Canola oil, for preparing the plastic wrap

Yield: 1 loaf

PREP TIME: 20 minutes

RISE TIME: Dough program plus 1 hour, plus 8 hours for the starter

COOK TIME: 35 minutes

Tuscan bread is probably as simple as bread can get—flour, water, yeast. The crust is pale; the shape of the loaf irregular; and the interior more tender than other "crusty" loaves. Also, the bread is deliberately bland, with no added salt, because it is meant to accompany strongly flavored meats, cheeses, and thick, rich sauces. Serve this loaf with chicken cacciatore or osso buco and use it to wipe the plate clean.

To make the starter: In the bucket of a bread machine, stir together the flour, water, and yeast until well combined. Set aside at room temperature for at least 8 hours, or overnight.

To make the dough: Add the water to the bucket, then the flour. Program the machine for Dough and press Start.

Line a baking sheet with parchment paper, lightly dust it with cornmeal, and set aside.

When the cycle is complete, transfer the dough to a lightly floured work surface and gently punch it down. Pull one side of the dough up to the center of the ball and gather the opposite side into the center, folding it slightly over the first side. Gather the third side and the fourth until you have a tight package.

Turn the dough over so the gathers are on the bottom and place both hands on the far side of the ball, cupping it, and gently drag the ball toward you, creating smooth tension on the surface. Rotate the ball a quarter turn and drag it again. Continue to rotate and drag until the dough is round and the surface is taut. Transfer the ball to the prepared baking sheet, cover with lightly oiled plastic wrap, and set aside to rise until doubled, about 1 hour.

Preheat the oven to 450°F (230°C).

Using a sharp knife, slash a square on the top of the loaf. Mist the bread with water.

Bake for 15 minutes, misting the loaf twice more. Reduce the oven temperature to 400°F (200°C). Bake the bread until deep brown and the internal temperature reaches 200°F (93°C), about 20 minutes more. Let the bread cool completely, then store in a sealed plastic bag at room temperature for up to 3 days, or freeze in a sealed plastic bag with the air pressed out for up to 2 months.

Pan Gallego

1 cup (240 ml) lukewarm water (100°F to 110°F, or 38°C to 43°C)

2½ tablespoons (38 ml) olive oil, plus more for preparing the baking dish and plastic wrap

1 teaspoon sugar

1¼ teaspoons sea salt

2½ cups (300 g) white bread flour, plus more for the work surface

½ cup (62.5 g) whole wheat flour

½ cup (64 g) rye flour

2¼ teaspoons active yeast

¼ cup (40 g) raw pumpkin seeds

2 tablespoons (18.75 g) raw sunflower seeds

Yield: 1 loaf

PREP TIME: 15 minutes

RISE TIME: Dough program plus 1 hour, 30 minutes

COOK TIME: 35 minutes

This Galician (Spanish) bread comes in many variations, but this one is simplified without a starter or the distinctive knot of dough on top. You can form the loaf with the knot, but it takes a bit of practice. The crust on this bread is thick and studded with seeds for an appetizing finish. Try to eat the loaf the same day, when the flavor and texture are best.

In the bucket of a bread machine, combine the water, oil, sugar, and salt. Add the flours and yeast. Program the machine for Dough and press Start.

When the machine signals, add the seeds.

Lightly coat a 9-inch (23 cm) round baking dish with oil and set aside.

When the cycle is complete, remove the dough from the bucket, shape it into a ball, and transfer to a lightly floured work surface. Pull one side of the dough up to the center of the ball and gather the opposite side into the center, folding it slightly over the first side. Gather the third side and the fourth until you have a tight package.

Turn the dough over so the gathers are on the bottom and place both hands on the far side of the ball, cupping it, and gently drag the ball toward you, creating smooth tension on the surface. Rotate the ball a quarter turn and drag it again. Continue to rotate and drag until the dough is round and the surface is taut. Transfer the ball to the prepared baking dish, cover with lightly oiled plastic wrap, and set aside to rise until doubled, 1 to 1½ hours.

Preheat the oven to 425°F (220°C) and place a pan on the lower rack. Add 2 or 3 ice cubes to that pan to create steam.

Bake the loaf until golden brown and the internal temperature reaches 190°F (88°C), 30 to 35 minutes. Let the bread cool completely, then store in a sealed plastic bag at room temperature for up to 6 days, or freeze in a sealed plastic bag with the air pressed out for up to 2 months.

Pumpkin seeds are incredibly nutritious. They are packed with antioxidants, fiber, magnesium, manganese, and iron. Use raw seeds rather than roasted because the roasted ones can cook too much when on the outside of the loaf, creating a slightly bitter taste.

Dutch Boule

1½ cups (360 ml) lukewarm water (100°F to 110°F, or 38°C to 43°C)

1½ teaspoons sea salt

1½ teaspoons sugar

1 teaspoon olive oil, plus more for the bowl and loaf

3 cups (360 g) white bread flour, plus more for the work surface and the loaf

2¼ teaspoons instant dry yeast, or bread machine yeast

Yield: 1 loaf

PREP TIME: 15 minutes

RISE TIME: Dough program plus 1 hour

COOK TIME: 45 minutes

Boule means "ball" in French and is a classic shape used for many loaves in this book, kind of like a slightly deflated ball. This recipe is simple, like many other crusty loaves, utilizing limited ingredients to produce golden perfection. The hint of sugar creates a deep gold caramelized crust and balanced flavor. Baking the bread in a Dutch oven ensures steam is trapped with the baking loaf, creating volume and full-bodied flavor.

In the bucket of a bread machine, combine the water, salt, sugar, and oil. Add the flour and yeast. Program the machine for Dough and press Start.

When the cycle is complete, transfer the dough to a lightly floured work surface. Fold one side of the dough over the center of the dough ball, turn the ball a quarter turn, and fold the next side over the center. Repeat with the remaining two sides creating a tight package.

Turn the dough over so the smooth side is on top and place it in a lightly oiled large bowl. Coat the top of the dough with oil, then cover with plastic wrap and a clean kitchen cloth. Set aside to double for 1 hour.

While the dough is doubling, preheat the oven to 450°F (230°C) and place a large 6-quart Dutch oven inside the oven for 45 minutes.

Transfer the risen dough to a lightly floured work surface and dust it with flour. Using your cupped hands, form the dough into a ball.

Remove the Dutch oven and place it on a heatproof surface. Very carefully place the dough in the hot pot, cover with the lid, and bake for 30 minutes. Remove the lid and bake for 15 minutes more until the bread is deep golden brown and has a lovely crust. Remove from the pot and set aside to cool completely. Refrigerate in a sealed plastic bag for up to 3 days, or freeze in a sealed plastic bag with the air pressed out for up to 2 months.

I have a preference for turning my dough onto a very lightly floured counter for forming into loaves, but there are differing opinions on whether this practice adds too much flour and ruins the bread. A very light dusting of flour has never wrecked any of my bread, but if you think you might be too generous with flour, use oil spray or a little melted butter instead. Spray the counter and your hands and shape the dough as you wish.

Circle Bread

1½ cups (360 ml) lukewarm water (100°F to 110°F, or 38°C to 43°C)

1 tablespoon (12.5 g) sugar

1¾ teaspoons sea salt

4 cups (480 h) white bread flour, plus more for the work surface

2¼ teaspoons instant dry yeast, or bread machine yeast

Canola oil, for preparing the bowl

Yield: 1 loaf

PREP TIME: 20 minutes

RISE TIME: Dough program plus 1 hour

COOK TIME: 35 minutes

Bread is one of those creations that can be formed into almost any shape. Some competitions involve bread doughs baked into baskets, fruit shapes, buildings, and other decorations. This simple circle is ideal for a stunning centerpiece on a holiday table filled with fresh fruit, or even flowers. The intricate braid looks like you spent hours forming it when it actually only takes a few minutes.

In the bucket of a bread machine, combine the water, sugar, and salt. Add the flour and yeast. Program the machine for Dough and press Start.

When the cycle is complete, turn the dough out on a lightly floured work surface and let it rest for 15 minutes. Divide the dough into 3 equal pieces and roll each into a smooth rope about 14 inches (35.5 cm) long. Firmly braid the ropes together, creating a long dough braid.

Line a baking sheet with parchment paper and place a 6-inch (15 cm) diameter ovenproof bowl in the center. Lightly coat the outside of the bowl with oil. Arrange the braid around the bowl overlapping the two ends, pinching them together to create a continuous circle.

Cover the entire structure with a clean kitchen cloth and set aside to rise for 45 minutes.

Preheat the oven to 400°F (200°C).

Bake the bread until golden and the internal temperature reaches 190°F (88°C), about 35 minutes. Remove the bowl from the center and the bread let cool completely. Store in a sealed plastic bag at room temperature for up to 3 days, or freeze in a sealed plastic bag with the air pressed out for up to 2 months.

Most recipes in this book, and in most bread books, tell you to let dough rise until doubled, but this volume increase can be difficult to determine by eyeballing the dough. Instead, push one or two fingers about 1 inch (2.5 cm) into the risen dough; if the indents disappear, the dough is not ready. If the marks remain, move on to the next step. This method is recommended only for the first and second rise, not once the dough has been formed into a finished loaf. You do not want fingermarks in the loaf after it is baked.

Classic Cottage Loaf

1¼ cups (300 ml) lukewarm water (100°F to 110°F, or 38°C to 43°C)

2 tablespoons (30 ml) olive oil

2 tablespoons (25 g) sugar

2 teaspoons sea salt

4 cups plus 2 tablespoons (495 g) white bread flour

2½ teaspoons instant dry yeast, or bread machine yeast

Yield: 1 loaf

PREP TIME: 10 minutes

RISE TIME AND COOK TIME:
2½-pound (1.1 kg)/French program

The first year I worked in a kitchen, I learned this recipe from a charming French chef named Francis, who wrapped kitchen towels around his waist and did a veil dance to encourage the bread to rise. I still, on occasion, when alone and baking bread, do a little shimmy to evoke his memory. We did not use a bread machine because this was in North Africa, but I think he would have approved of the efficiency of the device and the glorious crunchy crust it produces.

In the bucket of a bread machine, combine the water, oil, sugar, and salt. Add the flour and yeast. Program the machine for French, select Medium crust, and press Start.

When the loaf is done, remove the bucket from the machine. Let the loaf cool for 5 minutes, then turn the bucket upside-down and gently shake it to remove the loaf. Transfer to a wire rack to cool completely. Store in a sealed plastic bag at room temperature for up to 3 days, or freeze in a sealed plastic bag with the air pressed out for up to 2 months.

Cracked Wheat Seed Bread

½ cup (80 g) cracked wheat

1¾ cups (420 ml) hot water (180°F to 190°F, or 82°C to 88°C)

¼ cup (60 ml) melted butter

3 tablespoons (60 g) maple syrup

2 teaspoons sea salt

3 cups (360 g) white bread flour

1 cup (125 g) whole wheat flour

¼ cup (56.75 g) pumpkin seeds (pepitas)

2 tablespoons (20 g) flaxseed

2 tablespoons (16 g) sesame seeds

2½ teaspoons instant dry yeast, or bread machine yeast

Cracked wheat is precisely what it sounds like, whole wheat berries ground into smaller pieces, including the nutritious germ and bran layers. This ingredient adds outstanding texture to bread and an enjoyable nutty taste. Soaking the wheat is a crucial step to ensure it is soft enough to chew so you don't damage your teeth on hard pieces. You can use bulgur wheat instead of cracked wheat with similar results.

In the bucket of a bread machine, combine the cracked wheat and hot water. Let sit until it cools to about 100°F (38°C), about 1 hour.

Add the melted butter, maple syrup, and salt, then the flours, seeds, and yeast. Program the machine for Basic, select Light or Medium crust, and press Start.

When the loaf is done, remove the bucket from the machine. Let the loaf cool for 5 minutes, then remove the loaf from the bucket. Let the bread cool completely, then store in a sealed plastic bag at room temperature for up to 4 days, or freeze in a sealed plastic bag with the air pressed out for up to 2 months.

Yield: 1 loaf

PREP TIME: 15 minutes

RISE TIME AND COOK TIME:
2-pound (908 g)/Basic program, plus 1 hour

Country Loaf

1¾ cups (420 ml) lukewarm water (100°F to 110°F, or 38°C to 43°C)

2 teaspoons sea salt

1 teaspoon sugar

4¾ cups (570 g) white bread flour, plus more for dusting

1¼ teaspoons instant dry yeast, or bread machine yeast

Yield: 1 loaf

PREP TIME: 10 minutes

RISE TIME: Dough program plus 3 hours, 30 minutes

COOK TIME: 35 minutes

When you think of artisan bread—rustic, golden, and thick-crusted—this will be the bread that comes to mind. The crust has a gorgeous pattern of squares dusted with flour, and the interior texture has an open but relatively regular crumb. This loaf was the first one I made back in the '90s that "sang" to me when it came out of the oven. This distinctive crackling noise occurs when "wet" dough is cooked at a high temperature with added steam. When the baked bread cools, the crust contracts and cracks, "singing" until the process stops.

In the bucket of a bread machine, stir together the water, salt, and sugar to combine. Add the flour and yeast. Program the machine for Dough and press Start.

When the cycle is complete, transfer the dough to a large bowl, tucking the sides under to form a tight ball. Cover with plastic wrap and let rise for 2 hours.

Lightly flour a medium bowl. Deflate the dough slightly and gather the top edges into the center, pinching to seal them together. Place the dough, smooth-side down, in the floured bowl and sprinkle more flour over the top. Cover with a clean kitchen cloth and set aside to rise until doubled, about 1½ hours.

Place a baking sheet or pizza stone on the middle oven rack and place a large metal baking dish on the bottom rack. Preheat the oven to 500°F (250°C).

Lightly flour another baking sheet and invert the bread dough onto the prepared sheet. Using a sharp knife, score the top of the dough diagonally about 3 times in one direction and 3 times across the other direction to form square patterns.

Using a large spatula, slide the dough onto the preheated baking sheet in the oven and pour 2 cups (480 ml) of boiling water into the baking dish underneath.

Bake for 5 minutes. Reduce the temperature to 400°F (200°C) and bake the bread until golden brown and very crusty, about 30 minutes. Let the bread cool completely, then store in a sealed plastic bag at room temperature for up to 3 days, or freeze in a sealed plastic bag with the air pressed out for up to 2 months.

Vienna Bread

1 cup (240 ml) lukewarm water (100°F to 110°F, or 38°C to 43°C)

½ cup (120 ml) lukewarm milk (100°F to 110°F, or 38°C to 43°C)

2 tablespoons (25 g) sugar

2 tablespoons canola oil (30 ml), or melted butter

2 teaspoons sea salt

3½ cups (420 g) white bread flour, plus more for the work surface

2¼ teaspoons instant dry yeast, or bread machine yeast

Yield: 1 loaf

PREP TIME: 15 minutes

RISE TIME: Dough program plus 1 hour

COOK TIME: 30 minutes

Vienna bread is a delicious Austrian loaf similar to the more familiar French bread, except for the addition of sugar to the dough. Austria was the originator of the bread-baking technique of adding steam to the oven to create a sublime crust. If you want to create a truly classic Vienna bread, add 1 tablespoon malt and 1 egg to the wet ingredients for tenderness. I prefer a sturdy crust, so I omit the egg and butter from the recipe, although I sometimes brush the finished loaf with melted butter to enhance the flavor.

In the bucket of a bread machine, combine the water, milk, sugar, oil, and salt. Add the flour and yeast. Program the machine for Dough and press Start.

Line a baking sheet with parchment paper and set aside.

When the cycle is complete, turn the dough out onto a lightly floured work surface, gently deflate it, and form it into an oval loaf, using your hands in a cupping motion to rotate the dough, tucking the sides under to create a smooth, taut surface. Place the loaf on the prepared baking sheet. Using a sharp knife, cut 3 shallow diagonal slashes in the top of the loaf, cover with a clean kitchen towel, and set aside until doubled, about 1 hour.

Preheat the oven to 425°F (220°C).

Bake the loaf until golden, about 30 minutes. Transfer the loaf to a wire rack to cool completely. Store in a sealed plastic bag at room temperature for up to 3 days, or freeze in a sealed plastic bag with the air pressed out for up to 2 months.

Rustic German Bread

¾ cup (180 g) plain Greek yogurt

½ cup (120 ml) lukewarm water (100°F to 110°F, or 38°C to 43°C)

½ cup (120 ml) lukewarm milk (100°F to 110°F, or 38°C to 43°C)

1 tablespoon (15 ml) apple cider vinegar

1 tablespoon (20 g) honey

2 teaspoons salt

3 cups (360 g) white bread flour, plus more for the work surface and the loaf

1 cup (125 g) whole wheat flour

1 cup (128 g) rye flour

½ teaspoon (3 g) coriander seeds

½ teaspoon (1 g) aniseed

1¾ teaspoons instant dry yeast, or bread machine yeast

Cornmeal, for dusting

Yield: 1 loaf

PREP TIME: 10 minutes

RISE TIME: Dough program plus 1 hour, 30 minutes

COOK TIME: 40 minutes

After spending time in Germany at a corporate chef's retreat, I came home with 5 extra pounds (2.3 kg) from drinking what seemed like actual vats of beer at Octoberfest and a carefully written-out recipe for *bauernbrot*, or farmer's bread. This dense, flavorful loaf is the epitome of a perfect loaf of European-style bread—thick crusted, made with quality ingredients, and packed with flavor. Yogurt adds an interesting sour tang to the loaf, but you could add 1 cup (225 to 250 g) of sourdough starter instead to produce a similar result.

In the bucket of a bread machine, combine the yogurt, water, milk, vinegar, honey, and salt. Add the flours, seeds, and yeast. Program the machine for Dough and press Start.

Dust a baking sheet with cornmeal and set aside.

When the cycle is complete, turn the dough out on a lightly floured work surface and shape the dough into a round loaf, using your hands to tuck the bottom edges under the ball tightly.

Transfer the dough to the prepared baking sheet and lightly dust the top with flour. Cover the loaf with a clean kitchen cloth and let rise until doubled, 1 to 1½ hours.

Preheat the oven to 425°F (220°C).

Using a sharp knife, slash the loaf with 3 or 4 diagonal lines. Bake the bread until it sounds hollow when tapped (be careful; it will be hot!) and the internal temperature reaches 190°F (88°C), about 40 minutes. Let the bread cool completely, then store in a sealed plastic bag at room temperature for up to 3 days, or freeze in a sealed plastic bag with the air pressed out for up to 2 months.

Chapter Five

SOURDOUGH BREADS

SOURDOUGH STARTER

½ cup (62.5 g) whole wheat flour

¼ cup (60 ml) filtered water, or bottled water, plus more for feeding

All-purpose flour, for feeding

Day 1: In a glass bowl or large 4-cup (960 ml) jar, stir together the flour and water until a thick paste forms. Loosely cover the top with plastic wrap. Set aside in a warm spot for 24 hours.

Day 2: Check the starter for bubbles and a dark liquid on top called hooch. If you see the liquid, remove it. Re-cover the container and set aside for 24 hours more.

Day 3: Divide the starter in half and discard half of it. It will be hard to separate because of the stretchy texture. Stir in ¼ cup (60 ml) of water and ½ cup (62 g) of all-purpose flour until well combined. Loosely re-cover and set aside for 24 hours more.

Days 4, 5, and 6: Repeat this process—divide, discard half, and feed—for the next 3 days. You will notice bubbles and the starter rising and falling. When the starter falls, feed it.

Day 7: The starter should be about doubled by this point, bubbly, and ready to use. If not, continue to feed it. Test the starter by scooping out a spoonful and dropping it into water. If it floats, you are good to go!

After 7 days: Transfer the starter to a clean container and refrigerate. Continue to feed it as required.

For a rye starter, use rye flour in place of the whole wheat and all-purpose flours and follow the same process.

Sourdough Bagels

1 cup (225 to 250 g) sourdough starter, fed, active, and at room temperature

1½ cups (360 ml) lukewarm water (100°F to 110°F, or 38°C to 43°C)

2 tablespoons (40 g) honey

1 tablespoon (15 ml) canola oil, plus more for preparing the bowl and plastic wrap

2½ teaspoons sea salt

5 cups (600 g) white bread flour, plus more for the work surface

1 tablespoon (14 g) baking soda

1 large egg

1 tablespoon (15 ml) water

Sesame seeds, poppy seeds, caraway seeds, coarse sea salt, for topping (optional)

Yield: 12 bagels

PREP TIME: 30 minutes

RISE TIME: Dough program plus 4 hours

COOK TIME: 21 minutes

I did not attempt to make bagels until I had about five years as a professional chef under my belt, and I regret waiting that long. For some reason, this bread intimidated me—with its forming, rising, boiling, topping, and baking. Little did I know how simple the process really is once you know how to do it. Take the time to read the steps before starting (you should do this with any recipe) so you understand the timing and techniques. Soon, you will have trays of bagels rising all over your kitchen, and you will never buy a bagel again.

In the bucket of a bread machine, combine the starter, lukewarm water, honey, oil, and salt. Add the flour. Program the machine for Dough and press Start.

When the cycle is complete, transfer the dough to a lightly oiled large bowl. Cover the bowl with lightly oiled plastic wrap and set aside to rise for 3 hours, folding the dough over to deflate at least every hour.

Line a baking sheet with parchment paper and set aside.

Turn the dough out onto a lightly floured work surface, keeping as much air as possible in it. Cut the dough into 12 equal pieces and gently roll each piece into a ball with your cupped hands. Poke a hole through the center of each ball and widen the hole to about 1½ inches (3.5 cm) in diameter. Place the bagels on the prepared baking sheet, loosely cover with a clean kitchen towel, and set aside to rise for 1 hour.

Preheat the oven to 450°F (230°C).

Fill a large deep skillet about three-quarters full with water and place it over high heat. Add the baking soda and bring to a boil. Working 3 per batch, gently drop the bagels into the boiling water and boil for 1 minute, turning at 30 seconds. Using a slotted spoon, transfer the boiled bagels to the baking sheet and repeat until all the bagels are boiled.

In a small bowl, whisk the egg and water. Brush the tops of the bagels with the egg wash. Sprinkle the bagels with a topping of choice (if using).

Bake the bagels until golden brown, about 20 minutes. Let the bagels cool completely, then store in a sealed plastic bag at room temperature for up to 5 days, or freeze in a sealed plastic bag with the air pressed out for up to 2 months.

Sourdough Baguettes

2 cups (450 to 500 g) sourdough starter, fed, active, and at room temperature

1 cup (240 ml) lukewarm water (100°F to 110°F, or 38°C to 43°C)

1 tablespoon (12.5 g) sugar

2 teaspoons sea salt

4½ cups (540 g) white bread flour, plus more for the work surface

1½ teaspoons instant dry yeast, or bread machine yeast

Canola oil, for preparing the plastic wrap

Yield: 3 loaves

PREP TIME: 30 minutes

RISE TIME: Dough program plus 1 hour

COOK TIME: 25 minutes

The technique for creating these golden beauties is identical to the other baguettes in this book, so once you master the steps, you can create perfect loaves every time. Similar to sourdough loaves in general, the addition of the starter cuts the amount of yeast needed and adds that delightful tangy flavor. Sourdough baguettes are the base for my famous hero sandwiches served for the Super Bowl, or as a filling snack for my towering teenage boys after school and work. They eat a whole one each heaped with toppings, which is the reason this recipe makes three loaves—one leftover for my husband and me.

In the bucket of a bread machine, combine the starter, water, sugar, and salt. Add the flour and yeast. Program the machine for Dough and press Start.

Line a baking sheet with parchment paper and set aside.

When the cycle is complete, transfer the dough to a lightly floured work surface. Cut the dough into 3 equal pieces and form each piece into a ball.

Follow the baguette shaping technique on page 82.

Cover the baguettes with lightly oiled plastic wrap and set aside to rise, not quite double, about 1 hour.

Preheat the oven to 450°F (230°C). Place a large baking dish on the bottom oven rack.

Using a sharp knife, cut 4 diagonal slashes in the baguettes and place them in the oven. Place about 5 ice cubes in the baking dish and close the door. Bake the baguettes until deep golden brown, about 25 minutes. Let the baguettes cool completely, then store in a sealed plastic bag at room temperature for 1 day, or freeze in a sealed plastic bag with the air pressed out for up to 2 months.

Sourdough French Bread

1½ cups (337.5 to 375 g) sourdough starter, fed, active, and at room temperature

¾ cup (180 ml) lukewarm water (100°F to 110°F, or 38°C to 43°C)

2½ tablespoons (31.25 g) sugar

2 teaspoons sea salt

4 cups (480 g) white bread flour

1½ teaspoons instant dry yeast, or bread machine yeast

Yield: 1 loaf

PREP TIME: 10 minutes

RISE TIME AND COOK TIME:
2-pound (908 g)/Basic program

The crust on this bread sets it apart as a "French" bread with its distinctive crackle when sliced and deep brown color. You can finish this recipe in the oven by setting the bread machine for Dough and forming the finished product into a long loaf. Use the stretch and fold technique (page 21) to create structure for the freeform loaf. Let it rise for about 1 hour, or until doubled, then bake in a 400°F (200°C) oven until golden and the internal temperature reaches about 190°F (88°C), about 25 minutes.

In the bucket of a bread machine, combine the starter, water, sugar, and salt. Add the flour and yeast. Program the machine for Basic, select Light or Medium crust, and press Start.

When the loaf is done, remove the bucket from the machine. Let the loaf cool for 5 minutes, then turn the bucket upside-down and gently shake it to remove the loaf. Transfer to a wire rack to cool completely. Store in a sealed plastic bag at room temperature for up to 3 days, or freeze in a sealed plastic bag with the air pressed out for up to 2 months.

One complaint many people have about loaves cooked in the bread machine is their shape. You can get a dreaded sloping loaf or huge holes from the paddles. Don't be afraid to handle the dough when the kneading cycle is complete. Take the dough out when removing the paddles, shape it into a symmetrical loaf, and put it back in. This ensures an even rise and bake.

Traditional Sourdough Bread

2½ cups (562.5 to 625 g) sourdough starter, fed, active, and at room temperature

3 tablespoons (45 ml) lukewarm water (100°F to 110°F, or 38°C to 43°C)

3 tablespoons (45 ml) melted butter, cooled

1 tablespoon (20 g) honey

2 teaspoons sea salt

3½ cups (420 g) white bread flour

2 teaspoons instant dry yeast, or bread machine yeast

Take this recipe out of your culinary toolbox when you want to impress with a perfect sourdough loaf but do not have time for shaping and proofing bread for oven baking. For a visually appealing loaf, I sometimes wait for the last kneading cycle to finish, then pop out the paddles of the bread machine before the proofing cycle begins. This action means there are no holes in the loaf where you have to cut out the paddles because they bake in.

In the bucket of a bread machine, combine the starter, water, melted butter, honey, and salt. Add the flour and yeast. Program the machine for Basic, select Light or Medium crust, and press Start.

When the loaf is done, remove the bucket from the machine. Let the loaf cool for 5 minutes, then turn the bucket upside-down and gently shake it to remove the loaf. Transfer to a wire rack to cool completely. Store in a sealed plastic bag at room temperature for up to 3 days, or freeze in a sealed plastic bag with the air pressed out for up to 2 months.

Yield: 1 loaf

PREP TIME: 10 minutes

RISE TIME AND COOK TIME:
2-pound (908 g)/Basic program

San Francisco Sourdough Bread

1½ cups (337.5 to 375 g) sourdough starter, fed, active, and at room temperature

1 cup (240 ml) lukewarm milk (100°F to 110°F, or 38°C to 43°C)

2 tablespoons (25 g) sugar

2 teaspoons sea salt

4¼ cups (540 g) white bread flour, plus more for the work surface

2¼ teaspoons instant dry yeast, or bread machine yeast

Cornmeal, for dusting the baking sheet

Canola oil, for preparing the plastic wrap

Yield: 1 loaf

PREP TIME: 10 minutes

RISE TIME: Dough program plus 1 hour

COOK TIME: 30 minutes

Sourdough contains good bacteria called *Lactobacillus*, similar to healthy foods such as yogurt or kefir. The presence of these good bacteria is very beneficial for your gut, which, in turn, means a strong immune system. The sourdough process produces natural bacteria that can pre-digest the starches in grains, so people with gluten issues can often eat sourdough.

San Francisco is famous for sourdough bread, the way other cities are famous for baked products, such as New York for bagels. The starter from one famous San Francisco bakery is marketed as a continuous strain reaching back to 1849—fed and maintained all these years to produce fantastic bread. This version of sourdough bread is not a traditional recipe because it contains added yeast, but you can increase the distinctive sour flavor by creating and feeding a starter for months, rather than days, if you have room in your refrigerator.

In the bucket of a bread machine, combine the starter, milk, sugar, and salt. Add the flour and yeast. Program the machine for Dough and press Start.

Line a baking sheet with parchment paper, dust it with cornmeal, and set aside.

When the cycle is complete, remove the dough from the bucket, shape it into a rough ball, and transfer to a lightly floured work surface. Pull one side of the dough up to the center of the ball and gather the opposite side into the center, folding it slightly over the first side. Gather the third side and the fourth until you have a tight package.

Turn the dough over so the gathers are on the bottom and place both hands on the far side of the ball, cupping it, and gently drag the ball toward you, creating smooth tension on the surface. Rotate the ball a half turn and drag it again. Continue to rotate and drag until the dough is a smooth oval and the surface is taut. Transfer the loaf to the prepared baking sheet, cover with lightly oiled plastic wrap, and set aside to rise until doubled, about 1 hour.

Preheat the oven to 400°F (200°C).

Using a sharp knife, cut 3 diagonal slashes in the loaf. Bake until the loaf is golden brown, 25 to 30 minutes. Let the bread cool completely, then store in a sealed plastic bag at room temperature for up to 2 days, or freeze in a sealed plastic bag with the air pressed out for up to 2 months.

Soft White Sourdough Bread

¾ cup (168.75 to 187.5 g) sourdough starter, fed, active, and at room temperature

½ cup plus 1 tablespoon (135 ml) lukewarm milk (100°F to 110°F, or 38°C to 43°C)

1 large egg

3 tablespoons (45 ml) melted butter

2 tablespoons (25 g) sugar

1½ teaspoons salt

3 cups (360 g) white bread flour, plus more for the work surface

1½ teaspoons instant dry yeast or bread machine yeast

Canola oil, for preparing the loaf pan and plastic wrap

Yield: 1 loaf

PREP TIME: 10 minutes

RISE TIME: Dough program plus 45 minutes

COOK TIME: 40 minutes

I was not aware soft white sandwich bread existed until I had lunch at a friend's house when I was about seven years old—our sandwiches were presented on purchased Wonder bread. My house only had hearty rye, whole grain, and crusty European loaves because my Dutch mother thought store-bought white bread wasn't "real" bread. I still secretly agree with her. This soft, very white, golden-crusted loaf is as close to that premade bread as I will ever get when making my own. The interior is fluffy and almost melts in the mouth, but it still boasts a firm, buttery crust to satisfy my preference.

In the bucket of a bread machine, combine the starter, milk, egg, melted butter, sugar, and salt. Add the flour and yeast. Program the machine for Dough and press Start.

Lightly coat a 9 × 5-inch (23 × 13 cm) loaf pan with oil and set aside.

When the cycle is complete, transfer the dough to a lightly floured work surface. Form the dough into a log, pulling the sides of the dough under with cupped hands to create a smooth surface. Place the dough in the prepared pan and loosely cover it with oiled plastic wrap. Set aside until the dough rises about 2 inches (5 cm) above the rim of the pan, about 45 minutes.

Preheat the oven to 350°F (180°C).

Bake the bread until golden brown and the internal temperature reaches 200°F (93°C), 35 to 40 minutes. Let the bread cool completely, then store in a sealed plastic bag at room temperature for up to 3 days, or freeze in a sealed plastic bag with the air pressed out for up to 2 months.

Whole Wheat Sourdough Bread

1 cup (225 to 250 g) whole wheat sourdough starter, fed, active, and at room temperature

1 cup (240 ml) lukewarm water (100°F to 110°F, or 38°C to 43°C)

2 tablespoons (30 ml) melted butter

1 teaspoon sugar

1 teaspoon sea salt

2 cups (250 g) whole wheat flour

1 cup (120 g) white bread flour, plus more for the work surface

1 teaspoon instant dry yeast, or bread machine yeast

Canola oil, for preparing the loaf pan and plastic wrap

Yield: 1 loaf

PREP TIME: 10 minutes

RISE TIME: Dough program plus 1 hour, 30 minutes

COOK TIME: 40 minutes

The slightly nutty flavor of whole wheat flour pairs beautifully with tangy sourdough starter, creating a loaf that might become a family favorite. I like this bread toasted when making almond butter, honey, and banana sandwiches for my boys. It is firm enough to hold the heaps of ingredients, and the flavor seems to cut the sweetness a little. For a nice finish, brush the dough with an egg wash and sprinkle whole rolled oats all over it before baking.

In the bucket of a bread machine, combine the starter, water, melted butter, sugar, and salt. Add the flours and yeast. Program the machine for Dough and press Start.

Lightly coat a 9 × 5-inch (23 × 13 cm) loaf pan with oil and set aside.

When the cycle is complete, transfer the dough to a lightly floured work surface. Form the dough into a log, pulling the sides of the dough under with cupped hands to create a smooth surface. Place the dough in the prepared pan and loosely cover it with oiled plastic wrap. Set aside until the dough rises about 2 inches (5 cm) above the rim of the pan, 1 to 1½ hours.

Preheat the oven to 350°F (180°C).

Bake the bread until golden brown and the internal temperature reaches 205°F (96°C), about 40 minutes. Let the bread cool completely, then store in a sealed plastic bag at room temperature for up to 3 days, or freeze in a sealed plastic bag with the air pressed out for up to 2 months.

- -

There are very few things as tempting as a freshly baked loaf of golden bread. You will want to cut a slice immediately—but refrain. It takes several hours of cooling for the starches in the baked loaf to set and the water to move outward from the hot interior to the crust. Have you ever sliced bread straight from the oven and found it doughy or sticky, but a few hours later, a slice is perfect? This is the reason you need to be patient. Warm is fine; hot is a risk.

Oatmeal Sourdough Bread

1 cup (225 to 250 g) sourdough starter, fed, active, and at room temperature

1 cup (240 ml) lukewarm water (100°F to 110°F, or 38°C to 43°C)

½ cup (120 ml) lukewarm milk (100°F to 110°F, or 38°C to 43°C)

3 tablespoons (45 g) packed light brown sugar

2 tablespoons (30 ml) melted butter

1½ teaspoons sea salt

4 cups (480 g) white bread flour, plus more for the work surface

½ cup (64 g) rye flour

1 cup (156 g) rolled oats

Canola oil, for preparing the loaf pans and plastic wrap

Yield: 2 loaves

PREP TIME: 10 minutes

RISE TIME: Dough program plus 1 hour, 30 minutes

COOK TIME: 35 minutes

If you are a fan of Bircher muesli, this bread is for you! The distinct flavor of brown sugar–sweetened oats and the sourdough starter is very close to this Swiss breakfast classic. You can enhance the similarity by adding sunflower seeds, raisins, or dried cranberries to the dough when the machine signals, about ½ cup (weight varies) total. This bread is quite dense, so the extra ingredients will not spoil the texture.

In the bucket of a bread machine, combine the starter, water, milk, brown sugar, melted butter, and salt. Add the flours and oats. Program the machine for Dough and press Start.

Lightly coat two 9 × 5-inch (23 × 13 cm) loaf pans with oil and set aside.

When the cycle is complete, transfer the dough to a lightly floured work surface. Form the dough into 2 logs, pulling the sides of the dough under with cupped hands to create a smooth surface. Place the dough in the pans and loosely cover with oiled plastic wrap. Set aside to rise until doubled, about 1½ hours.

Preheat the oven to 350°F (180°C).

Bake the bread until golden brown and the internal temperature reaches 200°F (93°C), 30 to 35 minutes. Let the bread cool completely, then store in a sealed plastic bag at room temperature for up to 3 days, or freeze in a sealed plastic bag with the air pressed out for up to 2 months.

Pumpkin Sourdough Bread

For Leaven

½ cup (112.5 to 125 g) sourdough starter, fed, active, and at room temperature

1¼ cups (150 g) white bread flour

¾ cup (180 ml) lukewarm water (100°F to 110°F, or 38°C to 43°C)

¼ teaspoon active dry yeast

For Dough

2 cups (490 g) canned pumpkin

¼ cup (60 ml) lukewarm milk (100°F to 110°F, or 38°C to 43°C)

2 tablespoons (30 g) packed light brown sugar

2 tablespoons (30 ml) melted butter

1½ tablespoons (27 g) salt

3 cups (360 g) white bread flour, plus more for the work surface

Cornmeal, for dusting the baking sheet

Yield: 2 loaves

PREP TIME: 20 minutes

RISE TIME: 12 hours for leaven; Dough program plus 1 hour

COOK TIME: 25 minutes

This recipe looks complicated: starter, leaven, dough, rising, shaping, rising, and, finally, baking. You might be wondering what a leaven is as well. Simply put, it is a starter, but since the recipe also calls for a starter in the leaven, it seemed less confusing to give this component a different name. This extra boost of starter helps the pumpkin-dense dough rise to the level required. You will also notice using the leaven means there is no added yeast in the dough.

To make the leaven: In the bucket of a bread machine, stir together the starter, flour, water, and yeast until well combined. Cover and set aside overnight, or for at least 12 hours, at room temperature.

To make the dough: Add the pumpkin, milk, brown sugar, melted butter, and salt to the bucket. Add the flour. Program the machine for Dough and press Start.

When the cycle is complete, transfer the dough to a lightly floured work surface and punch it down. Divide the dough into 2 equal pieces and form each into a rough ball.

Pick up 1 dough ball and pull one side of the dough up to the center of the ball and gather the opposite side into the center, folding it slightly over the first side. Gather the third side and the fourth until you have a tight package.

Turn the dough over so the gathers are on the bottom and place both hands on the far side of the ball, cupping it, and gently drag the ball toward you, creating smooth tension on the surface. Rotate the ball a quarter turn and drag it again. Continue to rotate and drag until the dough is round and the surface is taut. Repeat with the remaining dough ball.

Line a baking sheet with parchment paper and lightly dust it with cornmeal. Place the dough balls on the prepared baking sheet at least 6 inches (15 cm) apart. Cover the dough with a clean kitchen towel and set aside to double, about 1 hour.

Preheat the oven to 425°F (220°C).

Using a sharp knife, slash an "X" in the top of each loaf. Bake until the loaves are golden brown, 20 to 25 minutes. Let the bread cool completely, then store in a sealed plastic bag at room temperature for up to 2 days, or freeze in a sealed plastic bag with the air pressed out for up to 2 months.

Sweet Citrus Sourdough Bread

1 cup (225 to 250 g) sourdough starter, fed, active, and at room temperature

½ cup (120 ml) lukewarm water (100°F to 110°F, or 38°C to 43°C)

½ cup (120 ml) lukewarm milk (100°F to 110°F, or 38°C to 43°C)

½ cup (160 g) honey

1 large egg

¼ cup (60 ml) melted butter

2 teaspoons sea salt

Zest of 1 orange

Zest of 1 lemon

4 cups (480 g) white bread flour

2¼ teaspoons instant dry yeast, or bread machine yeast

Yield: 1 loaf

PREP TIME: 10 minutes

RISE TIME AND COOK TIME:
2-pound (908 g)/Sweet program

A perfect balance of citrus and honey characterizes this lovely loaf. When you slice it, tiny flecks of orange and yellow are visible in the snowy white center of the bread. This is the ideal choice for golden French toast or bread pudding because of its built-in flavor and porous texture. To enhance the citrus element, add a couple tablespoons (30 ml) orange juice concentrate or freshly squeezed lemon juice to the wet ingredients.

In the bucket of a bread machine, combine the starter, water, milk, honey, egg, melted butter, salt, orange zest, and lemon zest. Add the flour and yeast. Program the machine for Basic, select Light or Medium crust, and press Start.

When the loaf is done, remove the bucket from the machine. Let the loaf cool for 5 minutes, then turn the bucket upside-down and gently shake it to remove the loaf. Transfer to a wire rack to cool completely. Refrigerate in a sealed plastic bag for up to 4 days, or freeze in a sealed plastic bag with the air pressed out for up to 2 months.

Light Sourdough Rye

1 cup (225 to 250 g) sourdough starter, fed, active, and at room temperature

1½ cups (360 ml) lukewarm water (100°F to 110°F, or 38°C to 43°C)

2 teaspoons sea salt

2¼ cups (270 g) white bread flour, plus more for the work surface

2 cups (256) rye flour

1 tablespoon (7 g) caraway seeds

1 teaspoon instant dry yeast, or bread machine yeast

Canola oil, for preparing the baking dish and plastic wrap

Yield: 1 loaf

PREP TIME: 10 minutes

RISE TIME: Dough program plus 1 hour

COOK TIME: 30 minutes

Rye bread and sourdough are a natural combination found in many Scandinavian countries, Russia, and Germany. This version is made a little blonder with a substantial amount of white flour rather than the majority being rye. Use any type of rye flour for this loaf, but white/light rye or medium rye is the best choice. Omit the caraway seeds if they do not suit your palate.

In the bucket of a bread machine, combine the starter, water, and salt. Add the flours, caraway seeds, and yeast. Program the machine for Dough and press Start.

Lightly coat a 9-inch (23 cm) round baking dish with oil and set aside.

When the cycle is complete, remove the dough from the bucket, shape it into a ball, and transfer to a lightly floured work surface. Pull one side of the dough up to the center of the ball and gather the opposite side into the center, folding it slightly over the first side. Gather the third side and the fourth until you have a tight package.

Turn the dough over so the gathers are on the bottom and place both hands on the far side of the ball, cupping it, and gently drag the ball toward you, creating smooth tension on the surface. Rotate the ball a quarter turn and drag it again. Continue to rotate and drag until the dough is round and the surface is taut. Transfer the ball to the prepared baking dish, cover the dish with lightly oiled plastic wrap, and set aside to rise until doubled, about 1 hour.

Preheat the oven to 425°F (220°C).

Using a sharp knife, cut 2 diagonal slashes in the loaf. Bake the loaf until golden brown and the internal temperature reaches 190°F (88°C), 25 to 30 minutes. Let the bread cool completely, then store in a sealed plastic bag at room temperature for up to 2 days, or freeze in a sealed plastic bag with the air pressed out for up to 2 months.

You can purchase sourdough starter in dehydrated form, rehydrate it, and create some wonderful bread. It is as simple as searching for a live sourdough starter on Amazon or other sites.

Dark Chocolate Rye Bread

2½ cups (562.5 to 625 g) rye starter, or regular sourdough starter, fed, active, and at room temperature

¼ cup (60 ml) lukewarm water (100°F to 110°F, or 38°C to 43°C)

¼ cup (20 g) unsweetened cocoa powder

3 tablespoons (45 ml) melted butter, cooled

2 tablespoons (30 g) packed light brown sugar

2 teaspoons sea salt

2½ cups (300 g) white bread flour

1 cup (128 g) rye flour

2 teaspoons instant dry yeast, or bread machine yeast

½ cup (90 g) mini semisweet chocolate chips

Yield: 1 loaf

PREP TIME: 15 minutes

RISE TIME AND COOK TIME:
2-pound (908 g)/Basic program

Bread is one of the most seductive foods in the world—its scent like a siren call. I try to eat bread in moderation, but this loaf is my willpower downfall. The deep, rich, almost bitter flavor with tiny bursts of sweet chocolate draws me in with every bite (I actually polished off half a loaf standing next to the counter one time). So, this loaf comes with a disclaimer: It is addictive.

In the bucket of a bread machine, combine the starter, water, cocoa powder, melted butter, brown sugar, and salt. Add the flours and yeast. Program the machine for Basic, select Light or Medium crust, and press Start.

When the machine signals, add the chocolate chips.

When the loaf is done, remove the bucket from the machine. Let the loaf cool for 5 minutes, then turn the bucket upside-down and gently shake it to remove the loaf. Transfer to a wire rack to cool completely. Store in a sealed plastic bag at room temperature for up to 5 days, or freeze in a sealed plastic bag with the air pressed out for up to 2 months.

Chapter Six

SWEET BREADS

Brioche

¾ cup (180 ml) lukewarm milk (100°F to 110°F, or 38°C to 43°C)

4 large eggs, at room temperature, beaten

3 tablespoons (37.5 g) sugar

1 teaspoon salt

4 cups (480 g) white bread flour

2¼ teaspoons instant dry yeast, or bread machine yeast

¾ cup (168 g) butter, cut into tablespoon-size (14 g) pieces, at room temperature

Canola oil, for preparing the baking sheet

1 large egg yolk

1 teaspoon water

Yield: 1 loaf

PREP TIME: 15 minutes

RISE TIME: Dough program plus 1 hour, plus 2 hours to chill

COOK TIME: 30 minutes

Brioche is a charming tender-crumbed bread whose name sounds like something enjoyed on a warm spring day sitting on a French patio sipping *le chocolat chaud* or rich coffee. Brioche is an enriched bread, packed with butter and eggs, so it has a lovely golden hue and spectacular slightly sweet taste. If you do not have time, you can make this bread entirely in the bread machine, omit the egg wash ingredients and set the machine to Basic and Light crust.

In the bucket of a bread machine, combine the milk, eggs, sugar, and salt. Add the flour and yeast. Program the machine for Dough and press Start.

When the second kneading cycle is 10 minutes in, add the butter, one piece at a time, letting it become mostly incorporated before adding the next. It should take about 4 minutes to add all the butter. Close the lid and let the Dough cycle continue until done.

When the cycle is complete, transfer the dough to a large bowl, tucking the sides under to form a tight ball. Cover the bowl with plastic wrap and refrigerate for 2 hours.

Remove the brioche dough from the refrigerator and form it into whatever shape you like. For a braided loaf, cut the dough into three equal pieces and roll with your hands to form long strands. Braid the strands firmly and tuck under the top and bottom ends to form a tight loaf.

Lightly coat a baking sheet with oil and place the loaf on the prepared sheet. Cover with plastic wrap and let rise until doubled, about 1 hour.

Preheat the oven to 375°F (190°C).

In a small bowl, whisk the egg yolk and water. Brush the loaf with the egg wash.

Bake the bread until golden and the internal temperature reaches 200°F (93°C), 25 to 30 minutes. Let the bread cool completely, then store in a sealed plastic bag at room temperature for up to 3 days, or freeze in a sealed plastic bag with the air pressed out for up to 2 months.

Challah

½ cup plus 1 teaspoon (125 ml) lukewarm water (100°F to 110°F, or 38°C to 43°C), divided

½ cup (120 ml) lukewarm milk (100°F to 110°F, or 38°C to 43°C)

¼ cup (60 ml) melted butter

¼ cup (80 g) honey

3 large eggs, divided

1½ teaspoons salt

4 cups (480 g) white bread flour, plus more for the work surface

2¼ teaspoons instant dry yeast, or bread machine yeast

Canola oil, for preparing the dough

Yield: 1 loaf

PREP TIME: 15 minutes

RISE TIME: Dough program plus 1 hour, 45 minutes

COOK TIME: 30 minutes

My mother's ancestors were Jewish but, by the time I was born, the lineage was diluted to about one-eighth due to intermarriage and many tragic losses during World War II. In my mother's sewing pattern and old picture-filled scrapbooks, there was a faded paper covered with spidery cursive writing outlining my great-oma's challah recipe. I have changed a few quantities and used butter instead of oil because I like the flavor and don't have a religious limitation on dairy products. You can use canola oil if you want to stay true to tradition.

In the bucket of a bread machine, combine ½ cup (120 ml) of water, the milk, melted butter, honey, 2 eggs, and salt. Add the flour and yeast. Program the machine for Dough and press Start.

When the cycle is done, transfer the dough to a large bowl, tucking the sides under to form a tight ball. Lightly coat the top of the dough with oil and cover the bowl with plastic wrap. Let rise until, doubled, about 1 hour.

Line a baking sheet with parchment paper and set aside.

Punch down the dough and transfer it to a lightly floured work surface. Cut the dough into 4 equal pieces and roll each into a 12-inch (30 cm)-long rope with the ends tapered. Lay out the ropes in parallel lines and pinch the ropes together at the top.

Starting with the strand at the far right, place it over the next strand to the left, under the next one, and over the strand furthest to the left. Repeat this pattern with the strand farthest to the right until the entire loaf is braided. Pinch the ends together and neatly under tuck each end. Transfer the loaf to the prepared baking sheet.

In a small bowl, whisk the remaining egg and remaining 1 teaspoon of water and brush the loaf with the egg wash. Set the loaf aside to rise for 45 minutes.

Preheat the oven to 350°F (180°C).

Bake the loaf until golden and the internal temperature reaches 200°F (93°C), 25 to 30 minutes. Let the bread cool completely, then store in a sealed plastic bag at room temperature for up to 3 days, or freeze in a sealed plastic bag with the air pressed out for up to 2 months.

Stollen

For Fruit and Nuts

¼ cup (36.25 g) raisins

¼ cup (37.5 g) currants

¼ cup (43.75 g) candied lemon peel (see opposite), finely diced

¼ cup (43.75 g) candied orange peel (see opposite), finely diced

¼ cup (36.25 g) finely chopped blanched almonds

¼ cup (60 ml) dark rum

For Dough

1 cup (240 ml) lukewarm milk (100°F to 110°F, or 38°C to 43°C)

½ cup (112 g) butter, at room temperature

½ cup (100 g) granulated sugar

2 large eggs

1 large egg yolk

(continued)

You might think a dessert bread certainly does not belong in an artisan bread collection, but the care and time traditional German bakers take with this recipe certainly qualifies it. Stollen is more than bread; it is often part of the Christmas celebration for many people. Instead of just dusting the bread with powdered sugar, you can brush the finished, still-warm loaf all over with melted butter and roll it in sugar, creating a sweet protective coating that preserves the bread and keeps it moist.

To make the fruit and nuts: In a medium bowl, stir together the raisins, currants, candied lemon peel, candied orange peel, almonds, and rum. Let soak at room temperature for at least 1 hour. Drain any remaining liquid from the mixture.

To make the dough: In the bucket of a bread machine, combine the milk, butter, sugar, eggs, egg yolk, lemon zest, vanilla, cardamom, cinnamon, and salt. Add the flour and yeast. Program the machine for Dough and press Start.

When the machine signals, add the drained fruit.

Check the dough as it kneads. If it seems too wet and does not pull away from the sides of the insert, add extra flour in tablespoons until the desired consistency is reached.

When the cycle is complete, transfer the dough to a lightly floured work surface and divide it in half. Press each piece of dough into an oval about 10 inches (25 cm) long. Fold the ovals in half lengthwise, pressing along the seam, creating a divot along the length.

(continued)

Did you know more than 2.5 million stollen are sold in Germany every year around Christmas? There is actually an official formula for professional bakers that stipulates for every 200 grams of flour there must be 60 grams of dried fruit and 30 grams of butter for the bread to be considered stollen. Stollen can have many different ingredients, including marzipan, walnuts, poppy seeds, and quark or cottage cheese.

1 tablespoon (6 g) lemon zest

2 teaspoons pure vanilla extract

½ teaspoon ground cardamom

½ teaspoon ground cinnamon

1 teaspoon sea salt

3½ cups (420 g) white bread flour, plus more for consistency and for the work surface

1 tablespoon (12 g) instant dry yeast, or bread machine yeast

Powdered sugar, for dusting

Yield: 2 loaves

PREP TIME: 15 minutes

RISE TIME: Dough program plus 1 hour

COOK TIME: 30 minutes

Line a baking sheet with parchment paper, place the dough on it, and set aside to rise until doubled, about 1 hour. Remove any visible raisins.

Preheat the oven to 350°F (180°C).

Bake the bread until golden and the internal temperature reaches 190°F (88°C), 30 to 35 minutes. Let the loaves cool for about 10 minutes, then dust with powdered sugar. Let the bread cool completely, then store leftovers, tightly wrapped in plastic wrap, in a cool place for up to 2 weeks, or freeze a sealed plastic bag with the air pressed out for up to 2 months.

Candied Citrus Peel

3 to 3½ cups (300 to 350 g) citrus peel, from lemons, limes, oranges, or grapefruit

2 cups (400 g) sugar

1 cup (240 ml) water

Yield: 3 to 3½ cups (525 to 612.5 g)

Cut the peel off the citrus fruit with a thin layer of pith, then julienne the peel. Place the peel in a medium-size saucepan and add enough water to cover by 2 inches (5 cm). Bring to a boil over high heat and boil for 5 to 6 minutes. Drain and repeat twice more, so you blanch the peel 3 times. Transfer the blanched peel to a bowl and set aside.

In the same saucepan, stir together the sugar and water. Bring to a boil over high heat. Add the blanched peel, reduce the heat to low, and simmer for about 1 hour until the peel looks translucent.

Place a wire rack over parchment paper and spread the peel on the rack to cool and dry. When the peel is dry, store in a sealed container in a cool place for up to 1 month.

Portuguese Sweet Bread

1½ cups (360 ml) lukewarm milk (100°F to 110°F, or 38°C to 43°C)

2 large eggs

½ cup (100 g) sugar

⅓ cup (80 ml) melted butter

1½ teaspoons salt

4 cups (480 g) white bread flour

2 teaspoons instant dry yeast, or bread machine yeast

Yield: 1 loaf

PREP TIME: 10 minutes

RISE TIME AND COOK TIME:
2-pound (908 g)/Basic program

My mother-in-law, Diane, visits a lovely local bakery in her city before making the five hour drive to see us in our rural wonderland. The visit is to pick up a few loaves of soft, sweet Portuguese bread because I love it. With this recipe, I can make my own any time inspiration strikes—and entirely in the bread machine. The recipe makes a large loaf, so you might end up with leftovers. Use them to create a decadent bread pudding or French toast. The subtle sweetness of this loaf is absolute perfection when soaked in beaten egg and fried to a crispy golden brown. Enjoy!

In the bucket of a bread machine, stir together the milk, eggs, sugar, melted butter, and salt to combine. Add the flour and yeast. Program the machine for Basic, select Light crust, and press Start.

When the loaf is done, remove the bucket from the machine. Let the loaf cool for 5 minutes, then turn the bucket upside-down and gently shake it to remove the loaf. Transfer to a wire rack to cool completely. Store in a sealed plastic bag at room temperature for up to 3 days, or freeze in a sealed plastic bag with the air pressed out for up to 2 months.

Anadama Bread

1 cup (240 ml) lukewarm water (100°F to 110°F, or 38°C to 43°C)

¼ cup (80 g) molasses

3 tablespoons (45 ml) melted butter

1 tablespoon (12.5 g) sugar

1½ teaspoons sea salt

4 cups (480 g) white bread flour, plus more for the work surface

½ cup (70 g) yellow cornmeal

2½ teaspoons instant dry yeast, or bread machine yeast

Canola oil, for preparing the loaf pans

Yield: 2 loaves

PREP TIME: 10 minutes

RISE TIME: Dough program plus 1 hour

COOK TIME: 40 minutes

If you look up traditional bread from the United States, you will find this slightly sweet cornmeal bread in New England. The bread's origin is a little unclear, as with many recipes, but people have been enjoying this fine-crumbed nutty-tasting creation for more than 150 years. This loaf is particularly delightful with sliced turkey and a tart cranberry mayo, so make sure you whip up a few loaves around Thanksgiving or Christmas to have on hand.

In the bucket of a bread machine, stir together the water, molasses, melted butter, sugar, and salt to combine. Add the flour, cornmeal, and yeast. Program the machine for Dough and press Start.

Lightly coat two 9 × 5-inch (23 × 13 cm) loaf pans with oil and set aside.

When the cycle is complete, transfer the dough to a lightly floured work surface. Divide the dough into 2 equal pieces and form each into a log, pulling the sides of the dough under with cupped hands to create a smooth surface. Place the dough in the prepared pans and loosely cover them with plastic wrap. Set aside until doubled, about 1 hour.

Preheat the oven to 350°F (180°C).

Bake the bread until golden brown and the internal temperature reaches 200°F (93°C), about 40 minutes. Let the bread cool completely, then store in a sealed plastic bag at room temperature for up to 3 days, or freeze in a sealed plastic bag with the air pressed out for up to 2 months.

Pumpkin Pie Bread

¾ cup (184 g) pumpkin purée

¾ cup (180 ml) lukewarm milk (100°F to 110°F, or 38°C to 43°C)

1 large egg

¼ cup (60 g) packed light brown sugar

3 tablespoons (45 ml) melted butter

1¼ teaspoons sea salt

½ teaspoon ground cinnamon

¼ teaspoon ground nutmeg

¼ teaspoon ground ginger

⅛ teaspoon ground cloves

3¾ cups (450 g) white bread flour, plus more for the work surface

2 teaspoons instant dry yeast, or bread machine yeast

1 large egg yolk

1 tablespoon water

Yield: 1 loaf

PREP TIME: 10 minutes

RISE TIME: Dough program plus 1 hour

COOK TIME: 30 minutes

The color of this bread alone makes it one of the prettiest loaves in this book, so the warm scent of spices and golden sweet squash isn't the only thing that will keep you coming back for another slice. This loaf will work just as well with mashed cooked sweet potato or butternut squash if canned or fresh pumpkin is not easily obtainable. Just use the substitute ingredients in the same amount without changing the recipe at all. Top the egg-washed bread with a scattering of hulled pumpkin seeds (pepitas) to complete the autumn theme and add a delightful crunch.

In the bucket of a bread machine, combine the pumpkin, milk, egg, brown sugar, melted butter, salt, cinnamon, nutmeg, ginger, and cloves. Add the flour and yeast. Program the machine for Dough and press Start.

Line a baking sheet with parchment paper and set aside.

When the cycle is complete, transfer the dough to a lightly floured work surface and cut it into 3 equal pieces. Roll each with your palms to form three 12- to 14-inch (30 to 35 cm)-long strands. Braid the strands firmly and tuck both the top and bottom ends under to form a tight loaf. Place the loaf on the prepared baking sheet, cover it with a clean kitchen cloth, and let rise until doubled, 30 minutes to 1 hour.

Preheat the oven to 350°F (180°C).

In a small bowl, whisk the egg yolk and water. Brush the loaf with the egg wash.

Bake the bread until golden and the internal temperature reaches 200°F (93°C), 25 to 30 minutes. Let the bread cool completely, then store in a sealed plastic bag at room temperature for up to 3 days, or freeze in a sealed plastic bag with the air pressed out for up to 2 months.

Hawaiian Sweet Bread

¾ cup (180 ml) lukewarm pineapple juice (100°F to 110°F, or 38°C to 43°C)

¼ cup (60 ml) melted butter

¼ cup (60 g) packed light brown sugar

1 large egg

1 large egg yolk

1¼ teaspoons salt

½ teaspoon pure vanilla extract

3 cups (360 g) white bread flour

2 teaspoons instant dry yeast, or bread machine yeast

Yield: 1 loaf

PREP TIME: 10 minutes

RISE TIME AND COOK TIME:
2-pound (908 g)/Sweet program

This recipe took me about four days to prepare because every time I bought fresh pineapple juice, my 18-year-old son would finish off the whole container in one colossal swig. I had to hide the juice in the back of the refrigerator behind the buttermilk, but it was well worth the subterfuge. The flavor of pineapple is subtle but recognizable, and the acid in the juice seems to create a tender, golden loaf. I sometimes add ½ cup (60 g) shredded sweetened coconut to the flour in this recipe for a real treat, or top the bread with melted butter and toasted almond slices after popping it out of the bucket.

In the bucket of a bread machine, combine the pineapple juice, melted butter, brown sugar, egg, egg yolk, salt, and vanilla. Add the flour and yeast. Program the machine for Sweet, select Medium crust, and press Start.

When the loaf is done, remove the bucket from the bread machine. Let the loaf cool for 5 minutes, then turn the bucket upside-down and gently shake it to remove the loaf. Transfer to a wire rack to cool completely. Store in a sealed plastic bag at room temperature for up to 3 days, or freeze in a sealed plastic bag with the air pressed out for up to 2 months.

Enriched breads have their own challenges because the added ingredients can impede the action of the yeast. Sugar attracts the water in the dough, leaving less hydration for the yeast, and fat can slow the yeast, so you will need to let the dough rise longer, even overnight, in the refrigerator. Enriched doughs are prone to collapse if overproofed because they are heavier than lean doughs. Observe the temperature of your proof carefully because too hot an environment, about 85°F (29.5°C) or higher, can purge butter from the dough.

Panettone

1 cup (240 ml) lukewarm milk (100°F to 110°F, or 38°C to 43°C)

1 large egg

1 large egg yolk

¼ cup (60 ml) melted butter

3 tablespoons (45 g) packed light brown sugar

1 tablespoon (6 g) orange zest

1 tablespoon (6 g) lemon zest

1¼ teaspoons sea salt

½ teaspoon aniseed

3 cups (360 g) white bread flour

2¼ teaspoons instant dry yeast, or bread machine yeast

½ cup (75 g) dried currants

½ cup (50 g) candied citrus peel (page 129)

Yield 1 loaf

PREP TIME: 15 minutes

RISE TIME AND COOK TIME: 2-pound (908 g)/Sweet program

Panettone often starts showing up in shops in late November, as the Christmas season starts to swing into action. This high, fruit-filled bread often looks dry and a little unpalatable sitting next to the blocks of fruitcake on the shelves, but this appearance is not accurate. Home-baked panettone is tender-crumbed, and its flavor offers a subtle layering of licorice, citrus, and tart fruit. You can bake this loaf in the oven instead of finishing it in the bread machine if you have a panettone mold (a high-sided baking dish), or use a clean large coffee can. You will have to do two additional rises (one in the refrigerator for about 10 hours) and bake the bread in a 350°F (180°C) oven for about 1 hour.

In the bucket of a bread machine, combine the milk, egg, egg yolk, melted butter, brown sugar, orange zest, lemon zest, salt, and aniseed. Add the flour and yeast. Program the machine for Sweet, select Medium crust, and press Start.

When the machine signals, add the currants and citrus peel.

When the loaf is done, remove the bucket from the bread machine. Let the loaf cool for 5 minutes, then turn the bucket upside-down and gently shake it to remove the loaf. Transfer to a wire rack to cool completely. Store in a sealed plastic bag at room temperature for up to 4 days, or freeze in a sealed plastic bag with the air pressed out for up to 2 months.

Sweet Cranberry Bread

2/3 cup (160 ml) lukewarm milk (100°F to 110°F, or 38°C to 43°C)

1/2 cup (120 ml) lukewarm water (100°F to 110°F, or 38°C to 43°C)

1 large egg

1/4 cup (50 g) sugar

3 tablespoons (45 ml) melted butter, softened

1 teaspoon salt

4 cups (480 g) white bread flour

2 teaspoons instant dry yeast, or bread machine yeast

1 cup (480 g) sweetened dried cranberries

Yield: 1 loaf

PREP TIME: 10 minutes

RISE TIME AND COOK TIME:
2-pound (908 g)/Sweet program

You might think cranberry bread is the same as raisin bread, just less sweet. Although this is undoubtedly true, cranberries also add pretty color to breads and other recipes. Cranberries are the fruit of evergreen vines or shrubs found in wetlands and cultivated bogs. Harvesting these bright red berries is done by flooding the crop area with about 1 foot (30 cm) of water, releasing the fruit from the vines with a harvester, then corralling the floating berries right on the water's surface and pumping them into crates or containers. It is a spectacle that is actually a tourist attraction in some areas of Canada and the United States.

In the bucket of a bread machine, combine the milk, water, egg, sugar, melted butter, and salt. Add the flour and yeast. Program the machine for Sweet, select Light or Medium crust, and press Start.

When the machine signals, add the cranberries.

When the loaf is done, remove the bucket from the machine. Let the loaf cool for 5 minutes, then turn the bucket upside-down and gently shake it to remove the loaf. Transfer to a wire rack to cool completely. Store in a sealed plastic bag at room temperature for up to 3 days, or freeze in a sealed plastic bag with the air pressed out for up to 2 months.

Tsoureki

2 cups (400 g) sugar

1 cup (240 ml) lukewarm milk (100°F to 110°F, or 38°C to 43°C)

3 large eggs, divided

½ teaspoon sea salt

¼ teaspoon almond extract

⅛ teaspoon ground star anise

5¼ cups (630 g) white bread flour, plus more for the work surface

1 tablespoon (12 g) instant dry yeast, or bread machine yeast

½ cup (112 g) butter, cut into tablespoon-size (14 g) portions, at room temperature

1 tablespoon (15 ml) water

Yield: 1 loaf

PREP TIME: 20 minutes

RISE TIME: Dough program plus 1 hour, 30 minutes

COOK TIME: 20 minutes

This is not a perfect traditional version of Greek Easter bread because it does not include the spices mastic and mahlab. These are not readily available in grocery stores, so I use almond extract and anise to get as close as possible to their taste. If you can get the spices, omit the substitute ingredients and use ¼ teaspoon of each spice, or ½ teaspoon of just one. Top the bread with sliced almonds for a beautiful finish.

In the bucket of a bread machine, combine the sugar, milk, 2 eggs, salt, almond extract, and star anise. Add the flour, make a well in the center, and add the yeast to it. Program the machine for Dough and press Start.

When the machine signals, add the butter, 1 tablespoon at a time, letting it become mostly incorporated before adding the next piece. It should take about 3 minutes to add all the butter. Close the lid and let the Dough cycle continue until done.

Line a baking sheet with parchment paper and set aside.

When the cycle is complete, transfer the dough to a lightly floured work surface. Divide the dough into 3 equal parts and roll each piece with your palms to create a 12-inch (30 cm)-long rope. Join the strands at the top and braid them to form the loaf, tucking the ends under tightly. Transfer the loaf to the prepared baking sheet and cover the dough with plastic wrap. Set aside to double, 1 to 1½ hours.

Preheat the oven to 375°F (190°C).

In a small bowl, whisk the remaining egg and water. Carefully brush the egg wash over the loaf.

Bake the bread until golden brown and the internal temperature reaches 200°F (93°C), about 20 minutes. Let the bread cool completely, then store in a sealed plastic bag at room temperature for up to 5 days, or freeze in a sealed plastic bag with the air pressed out for up to 2 months.

Traditional tsoureki has hard-boiled eggs baked right into the bread. These eggs are dyed red. Although standard food-grade dye can be used, red onion skins or beets create a beautiful vibrant color. If you try this lovely traditional preparation, don't worry if the dye stains the bread a little; it will still taste delicious.

Dark Chocolate Bread

½ cup (120 ml) lukewarm milk (100°F to 110°F, or 38°C to 43°C)

¼ cup (70 g) melted semisweet chocolate

3 tablespoons (15 g) unsweetened cocoa powder

2 large eggs

¼ cup (60 g) packed light brown sugar

¼ cup (60 ml) melted butter

1¼ teaspoons sea salt

3¼ cups (390 g) white bread flour, plus more for the work surface

1¾ teaspoons active yeast

Canola oil, for preparing the loaf pan

Yield: 1 loaf

PREP TIME: 10 minutes

RISE TIME: Dough program plus 1 hour

COOK TIME: 35 minutes

I have placed this bread in the sweet bread category because it shares many characteristic ingredients, such as eggs and butter, but the finished loaf is not very sweet. The semisweet chocolate does add a hint of flavor, but you might be reminded more of dark rye bread when you try the first slice. I use this bread when making shaved rare roast beef, Swiss cheese, and hot mustard sandwiches for my husband.

In the bucket of a bread machine, stir together the milk, melted chocolate, cocoa powder, eggs, brown sugar, melted butter, and salt to combine. Add the flour and yeast. Program the machine for Dough and press Start.

Lightly coat a 9 × 5-inch (23 × 13 cm) loaf pan with oil and set aside.

When the cycle is complete, transfer the dough to a lightly floured work surface. Form the dough into a log, pulling the sides of the dough under with cupped hands to create a smooth surface. Place the dough in the prepared pan and loosely cover it with plastic wrap. Set aside until doubled, about 1 hour.

Preheat the oven to 350°F (180°C).

Bake the bread until the internal temperature reaches 200°F (93°C), about 35 minutes. Let the bread cool completely, then store in a sealed plastic bag at room temperature for up to 3 days, or freeze in a sealed plastic bag with the air pressed out for up to 2 months.

I live in Northern Canada, where the temperatures are often well below zero, so my kitchen has no appropriate place for bread to rise except my oven. I have an electric oven, so I need to turn it on, but the pilot light in a gas oven often puts out enough heat to create the perfect environment. I turn on my electric oven to the lowest setting for about 3 minutes, then turn it off. If you have a thermometer in the oven, shoot for about 90°F (32°C) or lower. Place a dish filled with hot water on the lowest oven rack to keep the dough moist and place the covered bowl with your dough in the oven. Close the door and let it rise.

Chapter Seven

FLATBREADS, ROLLS, AND BAGELS

Grissini

¾ cup (180 ml) lukewarm water (100°F to 110°F, or 38°C to 43°C)

3 tablespoons (45 ml) olive oil

1 tablespoon (7.5 g) skim milk powder

1 teaspoon sugar

1¼ teaspoons sea salt

3 cups (360 g) white bread flour, plus more for the work surface

1½ teaspoons instant dry yeast, or bread machine yeast

3 tablespoons (45 ml) melted butter

¼ cup (36 g) sesame seeds

Yield: 24 breadsticks

PREP TIME: 15 minutes
RISE TIME: Dough program
COOK TIME: 22 minutes

Don't confuse these crisp breadsticks with the awful packaged dry-as-dust ones that sometimes show up in restaurants. Grissini is more like the crisp edges of a perfectly baked pizza without the toppings. Serve them alongside a tasty dip or on an antipasto platter to impress guests and family. You can sprinkle them with dried herbs or Parmesan cheese instead of sesame seeds for a different flavor.

In the bucket of a bread machine, combine the water, oil, skim milk powder, sugar, and salt. Add the flour and yeast. Program the machine for Dough and press Start.

Line 2 baking sheets with parchment paper and set aside.

When the cycle is complete, transfer the dough to a lightly floured work surface. Divide the dough into 24 equal pieces and gently stretch and pull each into a thin 10-inch (25 cm)-long rope. Divide the dough ropes between the prepared baking sheets, about 2 inches (5 cm) apart. Brush the ropes with melted butter and sprinkle with sesame seeds.

Preheat the oven to 375°F (190°C).

Bake the breadsticks until golden brown and crispy, 20 to 22 minutes. Let cool completely before serving. Store any leftovers in a sealed plastic container at room temperature for up to 5 days.

Grissini can trace its origin back to the 1670s, to a medicinal remedy for a sick little boy who happened to be Vittorio Amedeo II, the Duke of Savoy. The doctor requested something that would be digested easily, and a local baker stretched the traditional bread of Torino into thin, crispy breadsticks. The remedy worked, and the ill child eventually ruled all of Italy—and the breadsticks became popular in this country and beyond.

Soft Breadsticks

1¼ cups (300 ml) lukewarm water (100°F to 110°F, or 38°C to 43°C)

2 tablespoons (30 ml) olive oil

1 tablespoon (12.5 g) sugar

1 tablespoon (3.6 g) dried Italian seasoning

1½ teaspoons sea salt

3¾ cups (450 g) white bread flour, plus more for the work surface

2¼ teaspoons instant dry yeast, or bread machine yeast

2 tablespoons (30 ml) melted butter

¼ cup (25 g) grated Parmesan cheese

Yield: 24 breadsticks

PREP TIME: 20 minutes

RISE TIME: Dough program plus 30 minutes

COOK TIME: 15 minutes

Although hard breadsticks, Grissini (page 142), equal the classic Italian bread, I prefer these golden pillow-soft gems instead. The Parmesan cheese topping adds just the right amount of saltiness and looks lovely. The best part about this recipe is it makes two dozen sticks, and they keep well either at room temperature or frozen. If you freeze them, just pop them in 250°F (120°C) oven for 15 minutes to reheat.

In the bucket of a bread machine, combine the water, oil, sugar, Italian seasoning, and salt. Add the flour and yeast. Program the machine for Dough and press Start.

Line 2 baking sheets with parchment paper and set aside.

When the cycle is complete, transfer the dough to a lightly floured work surface. Divide the dough into 24 equal pieces and roll each into a 6-inch (15 cm)-long rope. Divide the ropes between the prepared baking sheets, about 2 inches (5 cm) apart. Loosely cover them with a clean kitchen cloth and let rise for 30 minutes.

Preheat oven to 350°F (180°C).

Bake the breadsticks until golden brown, about 15 minutes. Brush with melted butter and sprinkle with Parmesan cheese. Serve warm. Store any leftovers in a sealed plastic bag at room temperature for up to 2 days, or freeze in a sealed bag with all the air pressed out for up to 2 months.

Fougasse

- -

1¼ cups (300 ml) lukewarm water (100°F to 110°F, or 38°C to 43°C)

¼ cup (60 ml) olive oil, divided

1½ teaspoons sea salt

1 teaspoon dried oregano

1 teaspoon dried rosemary

1 teaspoon dried thyme

3 cups (360 g) white bread flour, plus more for the work surface

2¼ teaspoons instant dry yeast, or bread machine yeast

Coarse sea salt, for topping

Yield: 1 loaf

PREP TIME: 20 minutes

RISE TIME: Dough program plus 30 minutes

COOK TIME: 20 minutes

Fougasse is sometimes called French focaccia, but I find it to be crisper and the distinctly slashed shape does not lend itself to toppings, although the flavor can be similar depending on the herbs used. This bread is supposed to resemble an ear of wheat, and it can be pulled apart easily along the cuts. Fougasse is often served as an appetizer or placed in the center of a table to be enjoyed as an accompaniment to soup or a thick stew.

In the bucket of a bread machine, combine the water, 2 tablespoons (30 ml) of oil, the salt, oregano, rosemary, and thyme. Add the flour and yeast. Program the machine for Dough and press Start.

Line a baking sheet with parchment paper and set aside.

When the cycle is complete, transfer the dough to a lightly floured work surface. Flatten the dough into a large oval about 10 × 12 inches (25 × 30 cm). Transfer the oval to the prepared baking sheet. Using a pizza cutter, cut a slash down the middle of the oval lengthwise, leaving about 1 inch (2.5 cm) uncut at each end. Make 6 diagonal cuts on each side of the lengthwise cut, making a leaf shape, and pull apart the holes to widen them by about 1½ inches (3.5 cm).

Brush the dough with the remaining 2 tablespoons (30 ml) of oil and loosely cover with a clean kitchen cloth. Let rise for 30 minutes.

Preheat oven to 400°F (200°C).

Sprinkle the loaf with sea salt. Bake until golden brown and the loaf sounds hollow when tapped (be careful; it will be hot!), about 20 minutes. Transfer the bread to a wire rack to cool completely. Store in a sealed plastic bag at room temperature for up to 2 days, or freeze in a sealed bag with all the air pressed out for up to 2 months.

Classic Pizza Dough

1¾ cups (420 ml) lukewarm water (100°F to 110°F, or 38°C to 43°C)

3 tablespoons (45 ml) olive oil

2 teaspoons sugar

1 teaspoon sea salt

4½ cups (540 g) white bread flour, plus more for the work surface

2½ teaspoons instant dry yeast, or bread machine yeast

Yield: 3 (1-pound, or 454 g) dough balls

PREP TIME: 15 minutes

RISE TIME: Dough program plus 20 minutes to rest

COOK TIME: 12 minutes

Who knew making perfect pizza dough is this easy? If I knew this during university, I might not have lived on ramen noodles and peanut butter, not mixed together, thankfully. Since this dough freezes beautifully, keep a few pounds of dough on hand for those pizza moments in life.

In the bucket of a bread machine, combine the water, oil, sugar, and salt. Add the flour and yeast. Program the machine for Dough and press Start.

When the cycle is complete, transfer the dough to a lightly floured work surface. Divide it into 3 equal pieces and stretch the dough to the bottom of each ball, using your cupped hands to form a smooth surface. Use immediately, or store for later. Cover the dough and refrigerate it overnight, but punch it down before making pizzas because the dough will rise again. Or, place the dough in a sealed plastic bag, press the air out, and freeze for up to 2 months. Thaw the dough overnight in the refrigerator before using.

If using immediately, let the dough rest about 20 minutes or it will shrink back when you try to spread it out.

Preheat the oven to 450°F (230°C).

Spread the dough out on pizza pans or baking sheets into the desired shape (round or rectangular) using your hands. Top with your favorite sauce and toppings.

Bake until crispy and golden, 10 to 12 minutes.

When you take pizza dough out of the refrigerator, let it come to room temperature or it will be too hard to stretch. If you overwork the dough, the resulting crust will be hard and unpalatable. Do not use a rolling pin to roll the dough—think instead of the iconic pizza chef throwing the dough to stretch it. You don't have to throw yours, but, to ensure an airy crust, use your hands and knuckles to stretch the dough into the desired shape. If you find the dough shrinks back, let it rest longer to relax the gluten.

Bagels

1¼ cups (300 ml) lukewarm water (100°F to 110°F, or 38°C to 43°C)

2 tablespoons (30 g) packed light brown sugar

1 tablespoon (15 ml) canola oil

1½ teaspoons sea salt

4¼ cups (510 g) white bread flour, plus more for the work surface

1 tablespoon (12 g) instant dry yeast, or bread machine yeast

¼ cup (80 g) honey

Yield: 12 bagels

PREP TIME: 30 minutes

RISE TIME: Dough program plus 45 minutes

COOK TIME: 30 minutes

Bagels are one of those iconic foods that seem to define cities, like New York and Montreal—for good reason. Movie scenes and book chapters have been devoted to this chewy bread. This base recipe for bagels is more Montreal than New York, boiled in honey water for a sweeter finish. If you want a shinier crust and chewier texture, add 2 tablespoons baking soda instead of honey to the water.

In the bucket of a bread machine, combine the water, brown sugar, oil, and salt. Add the flour and yeast. Program the machine for Dough and press Start.

Line a baking sheet with parchment paper and set aside.

When the cycle is complete, transfer the dough to a lightly floured work surface, keeping as much air as possible in it. Cut the dough into 12 equal pieces and gently roll each piece into a ball with your cupped hands.

Poke a hole through the center of each ball and widen the hole until it is about 1½ inches (3.5 cm) in diameter. Place the bagels on the prepared baking sheet, loosely cover them with a clean kitchen towel, and set aside to rise for 45 minutes.

Preheat the oven to 425°F (220°C).

Fill a large deep skillet about three-quarters full with water and place it over high heat. Add the honey and bring to a gentle boil.

About 3 per batch, gently drop the bagels into the boiling water. Boil for 2 minutes, turning at 1 minute. Using a slotted spoon, transfer the boiled bagels back to the baking sheet and repeat until all the bagels are boiled.

Bake the bagels until golden brown, 20 to 22 minutes. Let the bagels cool completely, then store in a sealed plastic bag at room temperature for up to 5 days, or freeze in a sealed plastic bag with the air pressed out for up to 2 months.

Focaccia

1 cup (240 ml) lukewarm water (100°F to 110°F, or 38°C to 43°C)

½ cup plus 2 tablespoons (150 ml) olive oil, divided, plus more for preparing the bowl and baking sheet

½ teaspoon honey

½ teaspoon sea salt

2½ cups (300 g) white bread flour

2¼ teaspoons instant dry yeast, or bread machine yeast

1 tablespoon dried oregano

Yield: 1 flatbread

PREP TIME: 15 minutes

RISE TIME: Dough program plus 1 hour, 25 minutes

COOK TIME: 20 minutes

Focaccia is a staple in my house; we use it as a snack without any embellishments, cut into large squares for sandwiches, and as the base for incredible pizzas. I use day-old focaccia for my pizzas because they are a little firmer and hold up when topped with sun-dried tomato pesto, artichoke hearts, shredded kale, and a generous sprinkling of shaved Asiago cheese. Try oils infused with garlic, chile pepper, or herbs as the finishing oil, or use your favorite herbs instead of oregano.

In the bucket of a bread machine, stir together the water, ½ cup (120 ml) of oil, the honey, and salt to combine. Add the flour and yeast. Program the machine for Dough and press Start.

When the cycle is complete, transfer the dough to a large oiled bowl, tucking the sides under to form a tight ball, turning to coat with the oil. Cover with a clean damp kitchen cloth and let rise for 1 hour.

Preheat the oven to 450°F (230°C). Lightly coat a 9 × 13-inch (23 × 33 cm) baking dish with oil.

Transfer the dough to the baking dish and press it down evenly to the edges. Brush the top with the remaining 2 tablespoons (30 ml) of oil and sprinkle with the oregano. Use your fingertips to make indents all over the top, then set the dough aside to rise for 25 minutes until puffy.

Bake the focaccia until golden brown, 18 to 20 minutes. Serve warm or let cool completely, then wrap in plastic wrap and refrigerate for up to 2 days, or freeze for up to 1 month. Reheat from frozen in a 400°F (200°C) oven for 10 minutes.

The history of focaccia is not entirely clear, but this simple flatbread was made from water, flour, olive oil, and salt with natural leavening from wild yeast sources. This flatbread was cooked by Romans in a *focacius*, or fireplace, to produce bread daily.

French Rolls

For Starter

1¼ cups (150 g) white bread flour

¼ cup (31.25 g) whole wheat flour

¾ cup (180 ml) lukewarm water (100°F to 110°F, or 38°C to 43°C)

⅛ teaspoon active dry yeast

For Dough

¾ cup (180 ml) lukewarm water (100°F to 110°F, or 38°C to 43°C)

1¾ teaspoons sea salt

3 cups (360 g) white bread flour, plus more for the work surface and the buns

½ teaspoon instant dry yeast, or bread machine yeast

Canola oil, for preparing the bowl

For Egg Wash

1 large egg

1 tablespoon (15 ml) water

Yield: 8 rolls

PREP TIME: 15 minutes

RISE TIME: Dough program plus 1 hour, 45 minutes, plus 18 hours for the starter

COOK TIME: 15 minutes

Crusty rolls don't last long in my house. When baking these (usually in a double batch!), I sometimes freeze the raw dough balls, then thaw them in the refrigerator overnight before rising and baking in the morning. Be sure to freeze the rolls individually on a tray before transferring the balls to a sealed freezer bag for longer storage.

To make the starter: In the bucket of a bread machine, stir together the flours, water, and yeast until well combined. Cover the bucket with plastic wrap and set aside at room temperature for 12 to 18 hours.

To make the dough: In the bucket of a bread machine, combine the water and salt. Add the flour and yeast. Program the machine to Dough and press Start.

When the cycle is complete, gather the dough into a ball and place it in a large, lightly oiled bowl, turning to coat with the oil. Cover the bowl with plastic wrap and set aside to double, about 1 hour.

Line a baking sheet with parchment paper and set aside.

Turn the dough out onto a lightly floured work surface and divide it into 12 equal pieces. Form each into a roughly square shape, about 3 inches (7.5 cm) wide, and place on the prepared baking sheet. Dust the tops with flour and loosely cover the rolls with plastic wrap. Set aside to rise for 45 minutes.

To make the egg wash: In a small bowl, whisk the egg and water. Brush the tops of the rolls with the egg wash.

Preheat the oven to 450°F (230°C).

Bake the rolls until golden brown, 12 to 15 minutes. Transfer the rolls to a wire rack to cool completely. Store leftover rolls in a sealed plastic bag at room temperature for up to 4 days, or freeze in a sealed bag with all the air pressed out for up to 2 months.

Crusty Sandwich Rolls

For Starter

1 cup (120 g) white bread flour

½ cup (120 ml) lukewarm water (100°F to 110°F, or 38°C to 43°C)

¼ teaspoon active dry yeast

For Dough

1 cup (240 ml) lukewarm water (100°F to 110°F, or 38°C to 43°C)

1 tablespoon (12.5 g) sugar

1 tablespoon (15 ml) canola oil, plus more for preparing the bowl

1½ teaspoons salt

3¼ cups (390 g) white bread flour, plus more for the work surface

¾ teaspoon instant dry yeast, or bread machine yeast

For Egg Wash

1 large egg

2 tablespoons (30 ml) water

Yield: 12 rolls

PREP TIME: 15 minutes

RISE TIME: Dough program plus 3 hours, 30 minutes, plus 12 hours for the starter

COOK TIME: 25 minutes

Rolls are often overlooked when you first start baking bread because large loaves **seem** so dramatic and the epitome of culinary skill. Rolls are just smaller versions of the same recipe in most cases, so the satisfying crunchy crust and tender white interior of these rolls are still an accomplishment. The high oven temperature and egg wash are crucial for creating the right crust consistency, so do not skip that step.

To make the starter: In the bucket of a bread machine, stir together the flour, water, and yeast until well combined. Cover the bucket with plastic wrap and refrigerate for 8 to 12 hours.

To make the dough: Put the bucket in the machine and add the water, sugar, oil, and salt to the starter. Add the flour and yeast. Program the machine for Dough and press Start.

When the cycle is complete, gather the dough and place it in a lightly oiled large bowl, turning to coat with the oil. Cover the bowl with plastic wrap and set aside to rise for 2 hours.

Line a baking sheet with parchment paper and set aside.

Transfer the dough to a lightly floured work surface and divide it into 12 equal pieces. Form each into a ball using your cupped hands to create tight, smooth rolls. Place the rolls on the prepared baking sheet and loosely cover them with a clean kitchen cloth. Let rise for 1 to 1½ hours.

Preheat the oven to 425°F (220°C).

To make the egg wash: In a small bowl, whisk the egg and water until blended. Brush the rolls with the egg wash. Using a sharp knife, slash an "X" in the top of each roll.

Bake the rolls until golden brown, about 25 minutes. Let the rolls cool completely, then store in a plastic bag at room temperature for up to 3 days, or freeze in a sealed plastic bag with the air pressed out for up to 1 month.

Multigrain Kaisers

¾ cup (180 ml) lukewarm water (100°F to 110°F, or 38°C to 43°C)

2 tablespoons (30 ml) canola oil

1 large egg

1 tablespoon (12.5 g) sugar

1½ teaspoons sea salt

2 cups (240 g) white bread flour, plus more for the work surface

1 cup (132 g) multigrain flour

1¾ teaspoons instant dry yeast, or bread machine yeast

1 tablespoon (15 ml) milk

2 tablespoons (16 g) sesame seeds

Yield: 6 rolls

PREP TIME: 15 minutes

RISE TIME: Dough program plus 1 hour

COOK TIME: 15 minutes

This is a simplified version of a traditional kaiser roll, created without the intricate folded pinwheel shape on top. You can try to make the top in the classic design, but the rolls will taste the same and the straightforward slashed "X" saves time. If you prefer a plain kaiser, swap the multigrain flour for regular white or whole wheat flour in the same amount.

In the bucket of a bread machine, combine the water, oil, egg, sugar, and salt. Add the flours and yeast. Program the machine for Dough and press Start.

Line a baking sheet with parchment paper and set aside.

When the cycle is complete, transfer the dough to a lightly floured work surface. Divide the dough into 6 equal pieces and shape each into a ball using your cupped hands to tuck the edges of the dough under and create a smooth, taut surface. Place the rolls on the prepared baking sheet and loosely cover them with a clean kitchen cloth. Set aside to rise until doubled, about 1 hour.

Preheat the oven to 425°F (220°C).

Cut a shallow "X" in the top of each roll. Brush each roll with milk and sprinkle with sesame seeds. Bake the rolls until they are golden brown, about 15 minutes. Transfer to a wire rack to cool completely. Store left-over rolls in a sealed plastic bag at room temperature for up to 3 days, or freezer in a sealed bag with all the air pressed out for up to 2 months.

Tender Flatbread

1 cup (240 ml) lukewarm water (100°F to 110°F, or 38°C to 43°C)

2 tablespoons (30 ml) olive oil

1¼ teaspoons salt

1 teaspoon sugar

3 cups (360 g) white bread flour, plus more for the work surface

2 teaspoons instant dry yeast, or bread machine yeast

Yield: 6 flatbreads

PREP TIME: 15 minutes
RISE TIME: Dough program
COOK TIME: 25 minutes

Middle Eastern–style flatbreads probably push the definition of artisan bread, but you won't care about definitions when biting into the velvety soft layers of lightly browned bread. This method uses no oil when frying, and the finished product is perfect for sopping up dips and sauces or wrapping around almost any delectable filling. If you want to freeze the finished flatbread, place pieces of parchment between each piece so that they are easy to separate.

In the bucket of a bread machine, combine the water, oil, salt, and sugar. Add the flour and yeast. Program the machine for Dough and press Start.

When the cycle is complete, transfer the dough to a lightly floured work surface. Punch the air out of the dough and divide it into 6 equal pieces. Form each piece into a ball and roll them into ovals or rounds with a rolling pin, about ¼ inch (6 mm) thick.

Heat a large skillet over medium-high heat until very hot. Place the first flatbread in the skillet. Cook until it puffs, forms bubbles on the surface, and is golden in a few spots underneath, about 2 minutes. Flip and cook for 2 minutes more. Wrap the cooked flatbread in a clean kitchen towel and set aside. Repeat with the remaining dough. Serve warm.

Store leftovers in a sealed plastic bag at room temperature for up to 4 days, or freeze in a sealed bag, with parchment between each piece, with all the air pressed out for up to 2 months.

Flatbreads are thought to be the first type of bread every made by people, dating back thousands of years. Even more modern bread, such as pita, has a long history in the Middle East. Flatbread was used as currency in ancient Egypt, and it was placed in tombs to honor the dead.

Dutch Crunch Bread (Tiger Bread)

Unless you have a European bakery in your neighborhood, you probably have not had the pleasure of eating one of these stripy rolls. The interesting top pattern and texture come from the liberal application of a rice flour–based topping that melts and cracks as the rolls bake in a high-heat oven. I remember eating chocolate sandwiches on tiger bread, nibbling along the pattern lines until every last bite was consumed.

For Dough

¾ cup (180 ml) lukewarm water (100°F to 110°F, or 38°C to 43°C)

¾ cup (180 ml) lukewarm milk (100°F to 110°F, or 38°C to 43°C)

1 tablespoon (12.5 g) sugar

1 tablespoon (15 ml) canola oil

1¼ teaspoons sea salt

3 cups (360 g) white bread flour, plus more for the work surface

¼ cup (31.25 g) whole wheat flour

2¼ teaspoons instant dry yeast, or bread machine yeast

For Topping

1 cup (158 g) rice flour

¾ cup (180 ml) lukewarm water (100°F to 110°F, or 38°C to 43°C)

1 tablespoon (12.5 g) sugar

1 tablespoon (15 ml) canola oil

2¼ teaspoons instant dry yeast, or bread machine yeast

¼ teaspoon sea salt

To make the dough: In the bucket of a bread machine, stir together the water, milk, sugar, oil, and salt to combine. Add the flours and yeast. Program the machine for Dough and press Start.

Line a baking sheet with parchment paper and set aside.

When the cycle is complete, transfer the dough to a lightly floured work surface. Divide the dough into 8 equal pieces and roll each into a tight ball, cupping your hands under the pieces to ensure a taut surface. Place the balls on the prepared baking sheet, leaving at least 3 inches (7.5 cm) between the rolls. Loosely cover the rolls with a clean kitchen towel and set aside to rise for at least 20 minutes.

To make the topping and finish the bread: While the rolls rise, in a medium bowl, stir together the rice flour, water, sugar, oil, yeast, and salt until well combined. Set aside until bubbly.

Preheat the oven to 400°F (200°C).

Evenly divide the topping mixture among the rolls, spreading it thickly on top.

Bake the rolls until the crust is golden brown and cracked, 20 to 22 minutes. Remove the rolls from the oven and serve warm. Let leftovers cool completely, then store the rolls in a sealed plastic bag at room temperature for up to 4 days, or freeze in a sealed plastic bag with the air pressed out for up to 2 months.

Yield: 8 rolls

PREP TIME: 15 minutes

RISE TIME: Dough program plus 20 minutes

COOK TIME: 22 minutes

The traditional oil used in the topping is sesame oil, so use it instead of canola oil if you have it. Canola gives the bread a less exotic flavor but does not change the texture and appearance of the bread at all.

Chapter Eight

SEED, NUT, AND FRUIT BREADS

Barmbrack Bread

1 cup (150 g) dried currants

1 cup (145 g) raisins

1 cup (240 ml) boiling water

1 cup (240 ml) lukewarm milk (100°F to 110°F, or 38°C to 43°C)

½ cup (120 ml) plus 2 tablespoons (30 ml; optional) lukewarm water (100°F to 110°F, or 38°C to 43°C), divided

¼ cup (60 ml) melted butter

1 large egg, beaten

¼ cup (50 g) granulated sugar

2 teaspoons salt

1 teaspoon ground cinnamon

¾ teaspoon ground allspice

¼ teaspoon ground nutmeg

4 cups (480 g) white bread flour, plus more for the work surface

2 teaspoons dried lemon zest

2½ teaspoons instant dry yeast, or bread machine yeast

Canola oil, for preparing the loaf pans

Yield: 2 loaves

PREP TIME: 15 minutes, plus 30 minutes to soak the fruit

RISE TIME: Dough program plus 1 hour

COOK TIME: 40 minutes

Barmbrack comes from the Irish *bairín breac*: Bairín means a loaf and breac means speckled (here, raisins), so, a speckled loaf. This is one of my favorite breads. The scent of the rising dough is enough to draw others into the kitchen for a peek! When testing bread recipes, I often make the bread; test the texture, color, and taste; then discard the loaf because no one needs twenty deliciously warm loaves of bread in the house. But, this bread was consumed down to the last crumb by my teenage boys and husband—and one of them doesn't even like raisin bread.

In a medium bowl, stir together the currants, raisins, and boiling water. Set aside for 30 minutes at room temperature. Drain the fruit, pat it dry with paper towel, and set aside.

In the bucket of a bread machine, combine the milk, ½ cup (120 ml) of lukewarm water, melted butter, egg, sugar, salt, cinnamon, allspice, and nutmeg. Add the flour, lemon zest, and yeast. Program the machine for Dough and press Start.

When the machine signals, add the drained fruit. The dough should be soft. If it is too dry, add 2 tablespoons (30 ml) of warm water.

Lightly coat two 9 × 5-inch (23 × 13 cm) loaf pans with oil and set aside.

When the cycle is complete, transfer the dough to a lightly floured work surface and divide it in half. Fold each piece in half, tucking the edges under to produce a smooth top. Pull the loaf toward you, with your hands on the side farthest away, to create tension on the surface. Repeat with the second loaf. Place the dough in the prepared loaf pans, smooth-side up. Cover with plastic wrap and set aside until doubled, about 1 hour.

Preheat the oven to 400°F (200°C)

Bake the bread until browned on top, about 20 minutes. Loosely cover with aluminum foil. Bake for about 20 minutes more until the bread is cooked through and the internal temperature reaches 195°F (90.5°C). Let the bread cool for 15 minutes. Remove the loaves from the pans and let cool completely, then store in a sealed plastic bag at room temperature for up to 3 days, or freeze in a sealed plastic bag with the air pressed out for up to 2 months.

Raisin Pecan Bread

1 cup (240 ml) lukewarm water (100°F to 110°F, or 38°C to 43°C)

½ cup (120 ml) lukewarm milk (100°F to 110°F, or 38°C to 43°C)

3 tablespoons (45 ml) melted butter

3 tablespoons (37.5 g) sugar

1¼ teaspoons sea salt

1 teaspoon ground cinnamon

4 cups (480 g) white bread flour, plus more for the work surface

2¼ teaspoons instant dry yeast, or bread machine yeast

¾ cup (108.75 g) raisins

¼ cup (27.5 g) chopped pecans

Canola oil, for the bread

Yield: 1 loaf

PREP TIME: 10 minutes

RISE TIME: Dough program plus 1 hour

COOK TIME: 35 minutes

Raisin bread is one of those defining loaves—people either love it or hate it. I adore this recipe, especially toasted because the scent of cinnamon wafts through the house, and the sweetness of the raisins means no topping other than a little butter is required. You can find several raisin varieties at your local grocery store, but I like golden raisins because they are plump and still have a hint of grape flavor. Sultanas are nice, as well.

In the bucket of a bread machine, combine the water, milk, melted butter, sugar, salt, and cinnamon. Add the flour and yeast. Program the machine for Dough and press Start.

When the machine signals, add the raisins and pecans.

Line a baking sheet with parchment paper and set aside.

When the cycle is complete, transfer the dough to a lightly floured work surface.

Pull one side of the dough up to the center of the ball and gather the opposite side into the center, folding it slightly over the first side. Gather the third side and the fourth until you have a tight package.

Turn the dough over so the gathers are on the bottom and place both hands on the far side of the ball, cupping it, and gently drag the ball toward you, creating smooth tension on the surface. Rotate the ball a quarter turn and drag it again. Continue to rotate and drag until the dough is round and the surface is taut. Transfer the smooth dough ball to the prepared baking sheet.

Lightly coat the top of the dough with oil and cover with plastic wrap and a clean kitchen cloth. Set aside until doubled, about 1 hour.

Preheat the oven to 350°F (180°C).

Bake the bread until golden brown and the internal temperature reaches 190°F (88°C), about 35 minutes. Let the bread cool completely, then store in a sealed plastic bag at room temperature for up to 5 days, or freeze in a sealed plastic bag with the air pressed out for up to 2 months.

Whole Wheat Date Bread

1½ cups (360 ml) lukewarm water (100°F to 110°F, or 38°C to 43°C)

¼ cup (80 g) molasses

2 tablespoons (28 g) butter, melted and cooled

1 tablespoon (12.5 g) sugar

1 teaspoon salt

2 cups (250 g) whole wheat flour

1½ cups (180 g) white bread flour

2½ teaspoons instant yeast, or bread machine yeast

1 cup (145 g) chopped pitted dates

Yield: 1 loaf

PREP TIME: 10 minutes

RISE TIME AND COOK TIME:
2-pound (908 g)/Basic program

You might be reminded of a quick bread when you first slice this date-studded bread because it is very moist and has a pleasing sweetness. If you want a bit of crunch, add a ½ cup (55 g) chopped pecans with the dates. Look for Medjool dates whenever possible, for their caramel-like flavor and soft chewy texture. You might not know that these dates are actually fresh fruit, picked, cleaned, and packaged without drying, and it shows in the taste and texture.

In the bucket of a bread machine, combine the water, molasses, melted and cooled butter, sugar, and salt. Add the flours and yeast. Program the machine for Basic, select Light or Medium crust, and press Start.

When the machine signals, add the dates.

When the loaf is done, remove the bucket from the bread machine. Let the loaf cool for 10 minutes, then turn the bucket upside-down and gently shake it to remove the loaf. Transfer to a wire rack to cool completely. Store in a sealed plastic bag at room temperature for up to 3 days, or freeze in a sealed plastic bag with the air pressed out for up to 2 months.

Pick up a block of unsweetened date paste if whole fruit is not available or is too expensive. These date blocks are so densely pressed, you can easily cut them into ¼-inch (6 mm) cubes with a sharp knife.

Cranberry Honey Nut Bread

1 cup (240 ml) lukewarm water (100°F to 110°F, or 38°C to 43°C)

1 cup (240 ml) lukewarm milk (100°F to 110°F, or 38°C to 43°C)

3 tablespoons (45 ml) melted butter

1 tablespoon (20 g) honey

2 teaspoons sea salt

2¾ cups (330 g) white bread flour

1½ cups (187.5 g) whole wheat flour

2 teaspoons instant dry yeast, or bread machine yeast

¼ cup (30 g) dried sweetened cranberries

¼ cup (27.5 g) chopped pecans

¼ cup (31.25 g) chopped cashews

This lovely bread is made from start to finish in the bread machine with wonderful results, but it is even better when baked in the oven as a boule, a large round loaf. Simply set the dough program and, when completed, form the dough into a round loaf, let it rise, and bake in a 375°F (190°C) oven for 30 minutes. The crust has a fabulous thickness, and the exposed pecans toast beautifully adding a delightful crunch and rich flavor.

In the bucket of a bread machine, combine the water, milk, melted butter, honey, and salt. Add the flours and yeast. Program the machine for Basic, select Light or Medium crust, and press Start.

When the machine signals, add the cranberries and nuts. When the loaf is done, remove the bucket from the machine. Let the loaf cool for 5 minutes, then turn the bucket upside-down and gently shake it to remove the loaf. Transfer to a wire rack to cool completely. Store in a sealed plastic bag at room temperature for up to 4 days, or freeze in a sealed plastic bag with the air pressed out for up to 2 months.

Yield: 1 loaf

PREP TIME: 15 minutes

RISE TIME AND COOK TIME:
2-pound (908 g)/Basic program

Pain aux Noix

1½ cups (360 ml) lukewarm milk (100°F to 110°F, or 38°C to 43°C)

2 tablespoons (30 ml) melted butter

1 tablespoon (15 g) packed light brown sugar

1½ teaspoons sea salt

2¾ cups (330 g) white bread flour, plus more for the work surface

1 cup (125 g) whole wheat flour

2 teaspoons instant dry yeast, or bread machine yeast

1¼ cups (150 g) chopped walnuts

Yield: 1 loaf

PREP TIME: 10 minutes

RISE TIME: Dough program plus 1 hour

COOK TIME: 45 minutes

Pain aux noix is a very fancy (French) way of saying nut bread—in this case, walnuts. I usually avoid walnuts in baked goods because I find them slightly bitter when compared to butter-smooth pecans. In bread, this stronger flavor works because it is assertive enough to shine through whole grains and other ingredients. This loaf is very rustic looking with a thick dark crust and tender interior studded with walnut pieces. Enjoy with butter and honey for a continental breakfast experience.

In the bucket of a bread machine, combine the milk, melted butter, brown sugar, and salt. Add the flours and yeast. Program the machine for Dough and press Start.

When the machine signals, add the walnuts.

Line a baking sheet with parchment paper and set aside.

When the cycle is complete, transfer the dough to a lightly floured work surface and press the air out. Form the dough into a 12-inch (30 cm) long loaf, cupping your hands along the sides to tuck the dough under, creating a smooth, taut surface. Place the loaf on the prepared baking sheet and loosely cover it with a clean kitchen cloth. Set aside until doubled, about 1 hour.

Preheat the oven to 400°F (200°C).

Bake the bread until it sounds hollow when tapped (be careful; it will be hot!), about 45 minutes. Transfer the loaf to a wire rack to cool completely. Refrigerate in a sealed plastic bag for up to 4 days, or freeze in a sealed plastic bag with the air pressed out for up to 2 months.

Muesli Bread

1½ cups (360 ml) lukewarm water (100°F to 110°F, or 38°C to 43°C)

½ cup (120 g) packed light brown sugar

1 tablespoon (15 ml) canola oil

1½ teaspoons salt

3 cups (360 g) white bread flour, plus more for the work surface and the loaf

½ cup (78 g) rolled oats

2¼ teaspoons instant dry yeast, or bread machine yeast

¼ cup (37.5 g) raw sunflower seeds

¼ cup (30 g) dried cranberries

¼ cup (36.25 g) raisins

¼ cup (28.75 g) chopped raw hazelnuts

Yield: 1 loaf

PREP TIME: 10 minutes
RISE TIME: Dough program plus 1 hour
COOK TIME: 30 minutes

Instead of adding the different nuts and dried fruits individually, use a muesli mixture. There are usually oats in store-bought muesli, so omit that ingredient and add 1½ cups of cereal to the bread machine when it signals.

This dense little loaf reminds me of the bread I enjoyed while traveling through Europe, bursting with all sorts of interesting textures and tastes from the plentiful seeds, fruit, and nuts. It can be sliced very thinly and topped with buttery cheeses like Gouda and Brie or a thin layer of tart marmalade. The add-ins are just a guideline; experiment with your favorites in the same quantities.

In the bucket of a bread machine, combine the water, brown sugar, oil, and salt. Add the flour, oats, and yeast. Program the machine for Dough and press Start.

In a small bowl, stir together the sunflower seeds, cranberries, raisins, and hazelnuts until well combined. Set aside.

Line a baking sheet with parchment paper and set aside.

When the cycle is complete, transfer the dough to a lightly floured work surface.

Flatten the dough slightly and place the mixed nuts, seeds, and dried fruit in the center. Knead the bread a few times to incorporate the mixture without spreading it too far to the outside of the dough. Form the dough into a rough ball, then turn the dough until the smoothest side is on top.

Place both hands on the far side of the ball, cupping it, and gently drag the ball toward you, creating smooth tension on the surface. Rotate the ball a quarter turn and drag it again. Continue to rotate and drag until the dough is round and the surface is taut. Place the loaf on the prepared baking sheet. Lightly dust the loaf with flour, loosely cover it with a clean kitchen cloth, and set aside to rise for 1 hour.

Preheat the oven to 450°F (230°C). Place a baking dish on the lowest rack.

Add 2 or 3 ice cubes to the baking dish and place the baking sheet on an upper oven rack.

Bake the loaf until deep brown and the internal temperature reaches 190°F (88°C), about 30 minutes. Let the bread cool for at least 1 hour before cutting. Let cool completely, then refrigerate in a sealed plastic bag for up to 4 days, or freeze in a sealed plastic bag with the air pressed out for up 2 months.

Hazelnut Fig Bread

1½ cups (360 ml) lukewarm water (100°F to 110°F, or 38°C to 43°C)

½ cup (120 ml) lukewarm buttermilk (100°F to 110°F, or 38°C to 43°C)

¼ cup (60 ml) melted butter

¼ cup (80 g) honey

2 teaspoons salt

3 cups (360 g) white bread flour

1 cup (80 g) quick oats

½ cup (62.5 g) whole wheat flour

¼ teaspoon ground cinnamon

2 teaspoons instant dry yeast, or bread machine yeast

½ cup (57.5 g) chopped hazelnuts

¼ cup (36.25 g) chopped dried figs

I grew up with my Dutch mother. As a result, I was extremely popular in my school because we ate chocolate sandwiches when all the other kids had boring peanut butter. I was not aware my favorite spread, Nutella, was made with hazelnuts, but the marvelous rich taste of that nut is still top of my list. Hazelnuts are the star of this fruit-and-nut studded bread because, even in a relatively small amount, their flavor infuses every bite.

In the bucket of a bread machine, combine the water, buttermilk, melted butter, honey, and salt. Add the bread flour, oats, whole wheat flour, cinnamon, and yeast. Program the machine for Basic, select Light or Medium crust, and press Start.

When the machine signals, add the hazelnuts and figs.

When the loaf is done, remove the bucket from the machine. Let the loaf cool for 5 minutes, then turn the bucket upside-down and gently shake it to remove the loaf. Transfer to a wire rack to cool completely. Refrigerate in a sealed plastic bag for up to 4 days, or freeze in a sealed plastic bag with the air pressed out for up to 2 months.

Yield: 1 loaf

PREP TIME: 15 minutes
RISE TIME AND COOK TIME:
2-pound (908 g)/Basic program

Walnut Cob

2¼ cups (270 g) chopped toasted walnuts, divided

1¼ cups (300 ml) lukewarm water (100°F to 110°F, or 38°C to 43°C)

¼ cup (80 g) honey

¼ cup (60 ml) walnut oil

1½ teaspoons sea salt

3 cups (360 g) white bread flour, plus more for the work surface and the loaves

2 cups (250 g) whole wheat flour

2 teaspoons instant dry yeast, or bread machine yeast

Cornmeal, for dusting the baking sheet

Yield: 2 loaves

PREP TIME: 10 minutes

RISE TIME: Dough program plus 1 hour

COOK TIME: 30 minutes

Historically, cobs were small loaves made with denser flours, such as whole wheat or rye, by the lower classes in Britain hundreds of years ago. The addition of nuts is not traditional—they would have been too expensive—but walnuts are delicious. You get a triple layer of walnuts by using walnut oil, chopped nuts, and ground nuts. Pecans, cashews, and hazelnuts are superb substitutions.

In a food processor, pulse half the walnuts until finely ground.

In the bucket of a bread machine, combine the water, honey, oil, and salt. Add the flours, ground walnuts, and yeast. Program the machine for Dough and press Start.

When the machine signals, or the second kneading cycle starts, add the remaining chopped walnuts.

When the cycle is complete, transfer the dough to a lightly floured work surface and divide the dough into 2 equal pieces. Working with 1 piece at a time, pull one side of the dough up to the center of the ball and gather the opposite side into the center, folding it slightly over the first side. Gather the third side and the fourth until you have a tight package.

Turn the dough over so the gathers are on the bottom and place both hands on the far side of the ball, cupping it, and gently drag the ball toward you, creating smooth tension on the surface. Rotate the ball a quarter turn and drag it again. Continue to rotate and drag until the dough is round and the surface is taut. Repeat with the remaining dough.

Lightly dust a baking sheet with cornmeal and place the loaves on the prepared sheet. Loosely cover the loaves with plastic wrap and set aside to rise for 1 hour.

Preheat the oven to 350°F (180°C).

Lightly sprinkle the top of the loaves with flour. Using a serrated knife, cut an "X" in the top of each loaf about 1 inch (2.5 cm) deep.

Bake the loaves until deep brown and the internal temperature reaches 190°F (88°C), about 30 minutes. Let the bread cool for at least 1 hour before cutting. Refrigerate leftovers in a sealed plastic bag for up to 4 days, or freeze in a sealed plastic bag with the air pressed out for up to 2 months.

Spiced Apple Bread

1½ cups (360 ml) lukewarm water (100°F to 110°F, or 38°C to 43°C)

½ cup (120 ml) lukewarm milk (100°F to 110°F, or 38°C to 43°C)

2 tablespoons (30 g) packed light brown sugar

1 tablespoon (15 ml) melted butter

1½ teaspoons salt

½ teaspoon ground cinnamon

Pinch ground cloves

4½ cups (540 g) white bread flour, plus more for the work surface

2¼ teaspoons instant dry yeast, or bread machine yeast

1 cup (120 g) chopped dried apple

½ cup (55 g) chopped pecans

1 large egg

1 tablespoon (15 ml) water

Yield: 2 loaves

PREP TIME: 10 minutes

RISE TIME: Dough program plus 45 minutes

COOK TIME: 30 minutes

Dried fruit has an incredibly intense flavor, used to its advantage in this hearty bread, and will not produce soggy sections like fresh fruit chunks can. From the outside, you would not know these deep brown loaves are anything other than pretty artisan bread. However, when you cut your first slice, the scent of apples will be perceptible, reminding you of glossy, plump fruit and warm autumn days. Make turkey and cranberry mayo sandwiches on this bread after a festive holiday meal.

In the bucket of a bread machine, combine the lukewarm water, milk, brown sugar, melted butter, salt, cinnamon, and cloves. Add the flour and yeast. Program the machine for Dough and press Start.

When the machine signals, add the apple and pecans.

Line a baking sheet with parchment paper and set aside.

When the cycle is complete, transfer the dough to a lightly floured work surface and punch it down. Divide the dough into 2 equal pieces and shape each into a 12-inch (30 cm) long loaf with tapered ends. Using your cupped hands, draw the dough under the loaf creating a taut surface. Repeat with the second loaf. Place the loaves on the prepared baking sheet. Pick off any exposed pieces of apple. Cover the loaves with a clean kitchen cloth and let rise until doubled, about 45 minutes.

Preheat the oven to 375°F (190°C).

Using a sharp knife, cut 3 diagonal slashes in the top of each loaf. In a small bowl, whisk the egg and water. Brush the egg wash on both loaves.

Bake the bread until golden brown, about 30 minutes. Let the bread cool completely. Refrigerate in a sealed plastic bag for up to 3 days, or freeze in a sealed plastic bag with the air pressed out for up to 3 months.

Sunflower Seed Bread

1 cup (240 ml) lukewarm milk (100°F to 110°F, or 38°C to 43°C)

4 tablespoons (60 ml) melted butter, divided

1 large egg

3 tablespoons (45 g) packed light brown sugar

1 teaspoon sea salt

3 cups (360 g) white bread flour, plus more for the work surface

½ cup (78 g) rolled oats

2¼ teaspoons instant dry yeast, or bread machine yeast

½ cup (72.5 g) toasted unsalted sunflower seeds

Canola oil, for preparing the baking sheet and the bread

Yield: 1 loaf

PREP TIME: 10 minutes

RISE TIME: Dough program plus 1 hour

COOK TIME: 35 minutes

Many of the loaves in this book are quite fancy with interesting textures and tastes as well as pleasing shapes or crusts. This is an everyday loaf of bread, not flashy, but tasty to the last crumb. When you bake sunflower seeds into bread, they soften and quietly become part of the texture and taste. I like to use toasted seeds for extra flavor, but raw will work beautifully in a pinch. The seeds on the surface of the loaf will toast anyway, creating that desired taste.

In the bucket of a bread machine, combine the milk, 3 tablespoons (45 ml) of melted butter, the egg, brown sugar, and salt. Add the flour, oats, and yeast. Program the machine for Dough and press Start.

When the machine signals, add the sunflower seeds.

Lightly coat a baking sheet with oil and set aside.

When the cycle is complete, turn the dough out onto a lightly floured work surface. Pat the dough into a rough rectangle, about 10 × 6 inches (25 × 15 cm). Starting at a long end, tightly roll the dough to form a tight cylinder. Pinch to seal the seam and tuck the ends so they are smooth. Place the loaf on the prepared baking sheet and lightly coat the top of the dough with oil. Loosely cover the loaf with plastic wrap and a clean kitchen cloth. Set aside to double, about 1 hour.

Preheat the oven to 375°F (190°C).

Bake the loaf until golden brown and the internal temperature reaches 190°F (88°C), 30 to 35 minutes. Let the bread cool completely, then store in a sealed plastic bag at room temperature for up to 3 days, or freeze in a sealed plastic bag with the air pressed out for up to 2 months.

Seeded Whole Wheat Bread

1 cup (240 ml) lukewarm milk (100°F to 110°F, or 38°C to 43°C)

½ cup (120 ml) lukewarm water (100°F to 110°F, or 38°C to 43°C)

2 tablespoons (30 ml) olive oil

1½ tablespoons (18.75 g) sugar

1½ teaspoons sea salt

3 cups (360 g) white bread flour, plus more for the work surface

1 cup (125 g) whole wheat flour

2¼ teaspoons instant dry yeast, or bread machine yeast

¼ cup (56.75 g) pumpkin seeds (pepitas)

¼ cup (36 g) sesame seeds

2 tablespoons (18 g) poppy seeds

2 tablespoons (18 g) cornmeal

Olive oil cooking spray, for preparing the plastic wrap

Yield: 2 loaves

PREP TIME: 15 minutes

RISE TIME: Dough program plus 1 hour

COOK TIME: 25 minutes

My husband does not enjoy "seedy" bread because the seeds get stuck in his teeth. He had several teeth knocked out playing professional hockey, and little seeds find their way into painful places. So, I promised not to buy seedy bread—but I didn't say I wouldn't make it! The seeds can be anything you wish, including sunflower or flax, but keep the sesame seeds because they add a rich, nutty flavor.

In the bucket of a bread machine, combine the milk, water, oil, sugar, and salt. Add the flours and yeast. Set the machine for Dough and press Start.

When the machine signals, add the seeds.

Line a baking sheet with parchment paper, generously sprinkle it with cornmeal, and set aside.

When the cycle is complete, transfer the dough to a lightly floured work surface.

Cut the dough into 2 equal pieces and pat each into an oval about 8 × 5 inches (20 × 13 cm). Turn one piece so the longer side stretches away from you and fold it into overlapping thirds, similar to folding a letter before tucking it into an envelope. Use the heel of your hand to press the last edge closed firmly.

Flip the dough so the seam is on the bottom and shape it into an 8-inch (20 cm)-long log, scooping your hands under the dough from both sides to create surface tension on the loaf.

Place the shaped dough on one side of the prepared baking sheet and repeat with the remaining dough, placing it in the middle of the baking sheet, leaving room. Cover the dough with plastic wrap lightly coated with olive oil spray and set aside until doubled, about 1 hour.

Preheat the oven to 450°F (230°C).

Make four ½-inch (1 cm)-deep diagonal slashes in each loaf. Bake the loaves until browned on top and they sound hollow when tapped (be careful; they will be hot!), about 25 minutes. Let the loaves cool for 15 minutes. Remove the loaves from the pans and let cool completely, then store in a sealed plastic bag at room temperature for up to 3 days, or freeze in a sealed plastic bag with the air pressed out for up to 2 months.

Farro Whole Wheat Bread

1 cup (240 ml) lukewarm water (100°F to 110°F, or 38°C to 43°C)

½ cup (120 ml) lukewarm milk (100°F to 110°F, or 38°C to 43°C)

3 tablespoons (37.5 g) sugar

3 tablespoons (45 ml) canola oil

1¼ teaspoons salt

2 cups (250 g) whole wheat flour

1½ cups (180 g) white bread flour

¼ cup (30 g) skim milk powder

2 teaspoons instant dry yeast, or bread machine yeast

½ cup (50 g) cooked, cooled farro

½ cup (113.5 g) pumpkin seeds (pepitas)

Yield: 1 loaf

PREP TIME: 20 minutes
RISE TIME AND COOK TIME:
2 pound (908 g)/ Basic program

Farro is an ancient grain with a superb chewy texture and pleasant nutty taste that can enhance your bread, especially whole wheat or rye loaves. I use farro as a side dish and nutritious breakfast cereal because it is packed with nutrients. This grain is high in protein, fiber, iron, antioxidants, and magnesium. Cooked whole farro is my preference for this loaf, but you can use pearled or semi-pearled if you are looking for a shorter cook time.

In the bucket of a bread machine, combine the water, milk, sugar, oil, and salt. Add the flours, milk powder, and yeast. Program the machine for Basic, select Light or Medium crust, and press Start.

When the machine signals, add the farro and pumpkin seeds.

When the loaf is done, remove the bucket from the bread machine. Let the loaf cool for 10 minutes, then turn the bucket upside-down and gently shake it to remove the loaf. Transfer to a wire rack to cool completely. Store in a sealed plastic bag at room temperature for up to 3 days, or freeze in a sealed plastic bag with the air pressed out for up to 2 months.

Milk is often found in bread recipes, especially enriched bread. Milk powder is a popular ingredient in bread machine bread because it has all the benefits of liquid milk without adding extra hydration to the dough. Milk powder creates a soft, tender loaf because milk fat can impede gluten production. Milk powder can also increase browning of the crust because the milk sugars caramelize as the bread bakes.

Whole Wheat Flaxseed Bread

- - - - - - - - - - - - - - - - - - - -

1½ cups (360 ml) lukewarm water (100°F to 110°F, or 38°C to 43°C)

2 tablespoons (30 g) packed light brown sugar

2 tablespoons (30 ml) melted butter

1 teaspoon salt

3 cups (375 g) whole wheat flour

1¼ cups (150 g) white bread flour

¼ cup (28 g) ground flaxseed

2 teaspoons instant dry yeast, or bread machine yeast

Yield: 1 loaf

PREP TIME: 10 minutes

RISE TIME AND COOK TIME:
2-pound (908 g)/Basic program

Flaxseed is a staple ingredient in many bread recipes because it creates a more nutritious loaf high in healthy omega-3 fatty acids, protein, and fiber. The flaxseed in this recipe is ground, so you won't even notice it when cutting a slice for sandwiches, except for a hint of nuttiness. If you want more flaxseed in the recipe, increase the amount to ½ cup (56 g) and reduce the white flour to 1 cup (120 g).

In the bucket of a bread machine, combine the water, brown sugar, melted butter, and salt. Add the flours, flaxseed, and yeast. Program the machine for Basic, select Light or Medium crust, and press Start.

When the loaf is done, remove the bucket from the machine. Let the loaf cool for 5 minutes, then turn the bucket upside-down and gently shake it to remove the loaf. Transfer to a wire rack to cool completely. Store in a sealed plastic bag at room temperature for up to 5 days, or freeze in a sealed plastic bag with the air pressed out for up to 2 months.

Chapter Nine

HERB BREADS, CHEESE BREADS,

AND OTHER FLAVORED BREADS

Herb Butter Bread

1 cup (240 ml) lukewarm milk (100°F to 110°F, or 38°C to 43°C)

1 cup (240 ml) lukewarm water (100°F to 110°F, or 38°C to 43°C)

¼ cup (60 ml) melted butter, divided

2 tablespoons (40 g) honey

1½ teaspoons sea salt

4 cups (480 g) white bread flour, plus more for the work surface

1 tablespoon (weight varies) dried herbs, such as thyme, basil, oregano, tarragon, chives

1½ teaspoons instant dry yeast, or bread machine yeast

Canola oil, for preparing the dough

Yield: 1 loaf

PREP TIME: 10 minutes

RISE TIME: Dough program plus 1 hour

COOK TIME: 30 minutes

There is some truly spectacular bread in this book for your baking adventures, but this unassuming loaf is one of my absolute favorites. As a chef, I have an obsession with herbs—both their culinary and medicinal applications. So, a sweet, buttery, tender loaf of bread brimming with the taste and scent of herbs is perfection. I like using thyme, basil, and tarragon.

In the bucket of a bread machine, combine the milk, water, 3 tablespoons (45 ml) of melted butter, the honey, and salt. Add the flour, herbs, and yeast. Program the machine for Dough and press Start.

Line a baking sheet with parchment paper and set aside.

When the cycle is complete, turn the dough out onto a lightly floured work surface and gather it into a ball, pulling the dough into the center on all sides to create a smooth, tight ball.

Turn the dough over so the smooth side is on top and cup the dough all around, pulling it tightly under the ball to create surface tension. Place the loaf on the prepared baking sheet and lightly coat the surface of the dough with oil. Loosely cover with plastic wrap and set aside until doubled, about 1 hour.

Preheat the oven to 375°F (190°C).

Using a sharp knife, score the top of the dough diagonally about 3 times in one direction. Bake the bread until golden brown and it sounds hollow when tapped (be careful; it will be hot!), about 30 minutes.

Brush the loaf with the remaining 1 tablespoon (15 ml) of melted butter, then transfer to a wire rack to cool completely. Store any leftover bread in a sealed plastic bag at room temperature for up to 3 days, or freeze in a sealed plastic bag with the air pressed out for up to 2 months.

Sour Cream Herb Bread

¾ cup (180 ml) lukewarm whole milk (100°F to 110°F, or 38°C to 43°C)

¾ cup (172.5 g) sour cream, at room temperature

2 tablespoons (30 g) packed light brown sugar

1 tablespoon (15 ml) canola oil

1 teaspoon salt

½ teaspoon chopped fresh thyme leaves

½ teaspoon chopped fresh basil leaves

3¼ cups (390 g) white bread flour, plus more for the work surface

2¼ teaspoons instant dry yeast, or bread machine yeast

Canola oil, for preparing the loaf pan and loaf

Yield: 1 loaf

PREP TIME: 10 minutes

RISE TIME: Dough program plus 45 minutes

COOK TIME: 40 minutes

I call this faux sourdough bread because the addition of sour cream almost perfectly mimics the taste of real sourdough. Use full-fat cultivated sour cream for best results. Its thick creamy texture creates a tender almost cake-like crumb. The herbs in this recipe can be swapped for anything you have in the pantry, so experiment to find the combination you like best.

In the bucket of a bread machine, combine the milk, sour cream, brown sugar, oil, salt, thyme, and basil. Add the flour and yeast. Program the machine for Dough and press Start.

Lightly coat a 9 × 5-inch (23 × 13 cm) loaf pan with oil and set aside.

When the cycle is complete, transfer the dough to a lightly floured work surface. Form the dough into a log that will fit in the pan, using your hands to tuck the sides of the dough under, creating a smooth, taut top. Place the dough in the prepared pan and lightly coat the surface with oil. Loosely cover with plastic wrap and set aside to rise for about 45 minutes.

Preheat the oven to 350°F (180°C).

Bake the bread until golden brown and the internal temperature reaches 200°F (93°C), 35 to 40 minutes. Let the bread cool completely, then store in a sealed plastic bag at room temperature for up to 3 days, or freeze in a sealed plastic bag with the air pressed out for up to 2 months.

Bulgur Herb Bread

1 cup (240 ml) lukewarm water (100°F to 110°F, or 38°C to 43°C), divided

½ cup (70 g) bulgur

½ cup (120 ml) lukewarm buttermilk (100°F to 110°F, or 38°C to 43°C)

2 tablespoons (30 g) packed light brown sugar

1 tablespoon (15 ml) canola oil

1 teaspoon salt

½ teaspoon dried thyme

¼ teaspoon dried rosemary

¼ teaspoon dried parsley

3 cups (360 g) white bread flour, plus more for the work surface and the loaf

2¼ teaspoons instant dry yeast, or bread machine yeast

Yield: 1 loaf

PREP TIME: 10 minutes,
plus 30 minutes to soak the grains

RISE TIME: Dough program
plus 1 hour

COOK TIME: 30 minutes

Bulgur wheat is a common ingredient in Middle Eastern cuisine, and it is very easy to prepare and nutritious. Bulgur is cracked wheat groats that are parboiled and dried, so the cooking time is short, often just 30 minutes of soaking to produce a tender grain. Bulgur is high in fiber, containing all parts of the wheat kernel, as well as fiber, manganese, and iron. If you use leftover cooked bulgur in this bread, skip the soaking step at the beginning.

In the bucket of a bread machine, combine ½ cup (120 ml) of water and the bulgur. Let sit until the grains are softened, about 30 minutes.

Add the remaining ½ cup (120 ml) of water, buttermilk, brown sugar, oil, salt, thyme, rosemary, and parsley. Add the flour and yeast. Program the machine for Dough and press Start.

Line a baking sheet with parchment paper and set aside.

When the cycle is complete, transfer the dough to a lightly floured work surface. Form the dough into a rough ball, then turn the dough until the smoothest side is on the top. Place both hands on the far side of the ball, cupping it, and gently drag the ball toward you, creating smooth tension on the surface. Rotate the ball a half turn and drag it again. Continue to rotate and drag until the dough is an oval shape and the surface is taut. Place the loaf on the prepared baking sheet. Lightly flour the loaf, loosely cover it with a clean kitchen cloth, and set aside to rise for 1 hour.

Preheat the oven to 400°F (200°C).

Bake the loaf until golden brown and the internal temperature reaches 190°F (88°C), about 30 minutes. Let the bread cool for at least 1 hour before cutting. Refrigerate in a sealed plastic bag for up to 4 days, or freeze in a sealed plastic bag with the air pressed out for up to 2 months,

Semolina Thyme Bread

- -

For Sponge

1 cup (240 ml) lukewarm water (100°F to 110°F, or 38°C to 43°C)

1 cup (120 g) white bread flour

½ teaspoon instant dry yeast, or bread machine yeast

For Dough

¼ cup (60 ml) lukewarm water (100°F to 110°F, or 38°C to 43°C)

2 tablespoons (30 ml) melted butter

1½ teaspoons sea salt

1½ cups (255 g) semolina flour, plus more for dusting

1 cup (120 g) white bread flour, plus more for the work surface

1 teaspoon chopped fresh thyme leaves

½ teaspoon instant dry yeast, or bread machine yeast

Canola oil, for preparing the plastic wrap

Yield: 1 loaf

PREP TIME: 15 minutes

RISE TIME: Dough program plus 1 hour, plus up to 24 hours for the starter

COOK TIME: 35 minutes

Semolina is a flour made from durum wheat—the same flour used to make most pasta. This flour is coarser than standard wheat flour, golden in color, fragrant, and high in gluten, which is why pasta holds its shape when cooked. When added to bread, semolina imparts a sweet, almost fermented, flavor that is very pleasant when combined with the thyme. You can omit the chopped herb and still produce a very flavorful loaf.

To make the sponge: In the bucket of a bread machine, stir together the water, flour, and yeast until well combined. Cover the bucket with plastic wrap and set aside at room temperature overnight, or up to 24 hours.

To make the dough: Add the water, melted butter, and salt to the sponge. Add the flours, thyme, and yeast. Program the machine for Dough and press Start.

Line a baking sheet with parchment paper and dust it with semolina flour. Set aside.

When the cycle is complete, turn the dough out onto a lightly floured work surface and gather it into a ball, pulling the dough into the center on all sides to create a smooth, tight ball.

Turn the dough over so the smooth side is on top and cup the dough all around, pulling it tightly under the ball to create surface tension. Place the dough on the prepared baking sheet and loosely cover with oiled plastic wrap. Set aside until doubled, about 1 hour.

Preheat the oven to 400°F (200°C).

Using a sharp knife, score the top of the dough diagonally about 3 times in one direction.

Bake the bread until golden brown and it sounds hollow when tapped (be careful; it will be hot!), about 35 minutes. Transfer the loaf to a wire rack to cool completely. Store in a sealed plastic bag at room temperature for up to 3 days, or freeze in a sealed plastic bag with the air pressed out for up to 2 months.

Cardamom-Scented Bread

1 cup (240 ml) lukewarm milk (100°F to 110°F, or 38°C to 43°C)

1/2 cup (120 ml) lukewarm water (100°F to 110°F, or 38°C to 43°C)

3 tablespoons (45 ml) melted butter

2 tablespoons (40 g) honey

1 teaspoon sea salt

3¾ cups (450 g) white bread flour, plus more for the work surface

1 teaspoon ground cardamom

2¼ teaspoons instant dry yeast, or bread machine yeast

Canola oil, for preparing the loaf pan and dough

Yield: 1 loaf

PREP TIME: 10 minutes

RISE TIME: Dough program plus 45 minutes

COOK TIME: 25 minutes

If cardamom is not a regular resident of your spice shelf, you might be pleasantly surprised at what you have been missing when you inhale the scent of this bread. Cardamom is made from the pods of plants from the ginger family but is not as pungent as this other popular spice. Cardamom is citrusy, sweet, and almost minty. Its addition to bread creates a subtle scent rather than a discernible taste, so this recipe is an ideal way to become familiar with the spice without being overwhelmed by it.

In the bucket of a bread machine, combine the milk, water, melted butter, honey, and salt. Add the flour, cardamom, and yeast. Program the machine for Dough and press Start.

Lightly coat a 9 × 5-inch (23 × 13 cm) loaf pan with oil and set aside.

When the cycle is complete, transfer the dough to a lightly floured work surface. Roll the dough into a rectangle about 8 × 12 inches (20 × 30 cm). Starting at a long end, tightly roll the dough to form a cylinder and place it in the prepared loaf pan. Lightly coat the top of the loaf with oil and cover it with plastic wrap and a clean kitchen cloth. Set aside to rise until it rises about 1½ inches (3.5 cm) above the top of the pan, about 45 minutes.

Preheat the oven to 350°F (180°C).

Bake the bread until golden brown, about 25 minutes. Let the bread cool completely, then store in a sealed plastic bag at room temperature for up to 3 days, or freeze in a sealed plastic bag with the air pressed out for up to 2 months.

Potato Herb Bread

If you are looking for an airy loaf with a rich flavor, this is it. It is almost culinary magic that mashed potatoes can lighten the texture of bread, but this addition is also used in cakes and doughnuts to create that fabulous quality. It should be no surprise that this recipe has its origins in Ireland, a country famous for its potatoes. The best potatoes to use are starchy varieties such as Yukon Golds or russets.

1 cup (240 ml) lukewarm water (100°F to 110°F, or 38°C to 43°C)

1 cup (225 g) mashed potatoes, at room temperature

¼ cup (56 g) butter, melted and cooled

1 large egg

1 tablespoon (12.5 g) sugar

2 teaspoons chopped fresh thyme leaves

1 teaspoon chopped fresh oregano leaves

1½ teaspoons sea salt

4½ cups (540 g) white bread flour, plus more for the work surface

2½ teaspoons instant dry yeast, or bread machine yeast

Canola oil, for preparing the loaf pans

In the bucket of a bread machine, combine the water, mashed potatoes, melted butter, egg, sugar, herbs, and salt. Add the flour and yeast. Program the machine for Dough and press Start.

Lightly coat two 9 × 5-inch (23 × 13 cm) loaf pans with oil and set aside.

When the cycle is complete, transfer the dough to a lightly floured work surface. Divide the dough into 2 equal pieces and form each into a log that will fit in the pans. Place the dough in the prepared pans and loosely cover them with plastic wrap. Set aside until doubled, about 1 hour.

Preheat the oven to 350°F (180°C).

Bake the bread until golden brown and the internal temperature reaches 200°F (93°C), 40 to 45 minutes. If the bread browns too quickly, loosely cover the pans with aluminum foil. Let the bread cool completely, then store in a sealed plastic bag for up to 3 days, or freeze in a sealed plastic bag with the air pressed out for up to 2 months.

Yield: 2 loaves

PREP TIME: 10 minutes

RISE TIME: Dough program plus 1 hour

COOK TIME: 45 minutes

If you do not have mashed potatoes handy for this tender bread, whip up a batch from instant potato flakes. Make the mashed potatoes as directed by the package, adding a little less liquid for a firmer finished mash. Set aside to cool completely before adding to the recipe.

Black Pepper Parmesan Bread

1¾ cups (420 ml) lukewarm water (100°F to 110°F, or 38°C to 43°C)

1¾ teaspoons sea salt

1 teaspoon freshly cracked black pepper

3½ cups (420 g) white bread flour, plus more for the work surface

1½ teaspoons instant dry yeast

Canola oil, for preparing the bowl

1 tablespoon (9 g) cornmeal, plus more as needed

½ cup (50 g) shredded Parmesan cheese

Yield: 1 loaf

PREP TIME: 10 minutes

RISE TIME: Dough program plus 2 hours

COOK TIME: 30 minutes

Parmesan cheese is a popular bread topping; it bakes up golden brown and has a rich, nutty flavor. Parmesan has come from an area in Italy, called Parma, for more than 800 years. This cheese was renamed Parmigiano-Reggiano in the 1950s and only receives this name if it conforms to the Protected Designation of Origin (PDO) standards for Parmigiano-Reggiano.

Black pepper might seem like a humble spice, but this indigenous Indian plant was once one of the most expensive trading commodities in the world, traveling the 4,000 miles (6,437 km) of hard trail on the Silk Road from Asia to Europe. Pepper adds a satisfying hit to this bread but is not overwhelming. Use freshly cracked black pepper, not ground, for best results. Crack it yourself using the bottom of a skillet or a spice grinder.

In the bucket of a bread machine, combine the water, salt, and pepper. Add the flour and yeast. Program the machine for Dough and press Start.

When the cycle is complete, transfer the dough to a large oiled bowl, turning to coat with the oil, and tucking under the sides to form a tight ball. Cover the bowl with plastic wrap and let rise for 1 hour.

Dust a baking sheet with cornmeal and set aside.

Punch down the dough and turn it out on a lightly floured work surface. Pat the dough into a rough square, then fold one side into the center. Turn the dough a quarter turn and fold another side into the center. Repeat with the remaining two sides, creating a tight package.

Turn the dough over so the gathers are on the bottom and use your hands to pull the dough under the ball, creating a smooth surface. Place the loaf on the prepared baking sheet. Dust the top of the loaf with cornmeal and cover it with a clean kitchen cloth. Set aside to rise until doubled, about 1 hour.

Preheat the oven to 450°F (230°C).

Using a sharp knife, score the top of the dough diagonally about 3 times in one direction and sprinkle with Parmesan cheese.

Bake the bread until golden brown and crusty, about 30 minutes. Let the bread cool completely, then store in a sealed plastic bag at room temperature for up to 5 days, or freeze in a sealed plastic bag with the air pressed out for up to 2 months.

Cheddar Beer Bread

1 (12-ounce, or 360 ml) bottle of beer, at room temperature

2 tablespoons (30 ml) melted butter, cooled

2 tablespoons (25 g) granulated sugar

1½ teaspoons sea salt

4 cups (480 g) white bread flour

1½ cups (172.5 g) shredded Cheddar cheese, divided

1½ teaspoons instant dry yeast, or bread machine yeast

Yield: 1 loaf

PREP TIME: 10 minutes
RISE TIME: Dough program plus 1 hour
COOK TIME: 30 minutes

You can use nonalcoholic beer in this recipe but you will have to increase the yeast to 2¼ teaspoons to get the correct rise in the finished bread. Choose a darker "beer" for the best flavor.

When watching me put together yet another bread recipe, my husband came to full alert when he realized I was taking his last beer for baking. He might have forgiven me if I drank the beverage, but pouring it into my bread maker was almost criminal. The addition of sharp Cheddar seemed to lessen the offense and, when he tried his first bite of the finished loaf, I was completely exonerated. Beer, cheese, and bread— what could be better?

In the bucket of a bread machine, combine the beer, melted butter, sugar, and salt.

In a medium bowl, toss together the flour and 1 cup (115 g) of Cheddar, then add it to the bucket. Make a well in the ingredients and add the yeast to it. Program the machine for Dough and press Start.

Line a baking sheet with parchment paper and set aside.

When the cycle is complete, turn the dough out onto a smooth surface and gather it into a ball, pulling the dough into the center on all sides to create a smooth, tight top.

Turn the dough over so the smooth side is on top and cup the dough all around, pulling the dough tightly under the ball to create surface tension. Place the dough on the prepared baking sheet and loosely cover with plastic wrap. Set aside until doubled, about 1 hour.

Preheat the oven to 375°F (190°C).

Using a sharp knife, score the top of the dough diagonally about 3 times in one direction and 3 times across the others to form square patterns. Sprinkle with the remaining ½ cup (57.5 g) of Cheddar.

Bake the bread until golden brown and it sounds hollow when tapped (be careful; it will be hot!), about 30 minutes. Transfer the loaf to a wire rack to cool completely. Store leftovers in a sealed plastic bag at room temperature for up to 3 days, or freeze in a sealed plastic bag with the air pressed out for up to 2 months.

Cheesy Bacon Bread

¾ cup (180 ml) lukewarm milk (100°F to 110°F, or 38°C to 43°C)

2 tablespoons (40 g) honey

1 tablespoon (15 ml) melted butter

2 teaspoons salt

4 cups (480 g) white bread flour

¾ cup (86.25 g) shredded Gouda cheese, or Swiss cheese

¾ cup (60 g) chopped cooked bacon

2½ teaspoons instant dry yeast, or bread machine yeast

Yield: 1 loaf

PREP TIME: 15 minutes

RISE TIME AND COOK TIME:
2-pound (908 g)/Basic program

You might envision the finished loaf from this recipe as white cheesy-tasting bread studded with bacon chunks, but the kneading process seems to chop the bacon into tiny pieces that get incorporated throughout the dough. So, every bite of the interior is both cheesy and bacon-y. If you want chunks, wait until the machine signals before adding the chopped bacon or use a more robust product, such as pancetta.

In the bucket of a bread machine, combine the milk, honey, melted butter, and salt.

In a large bowl, toss together the flour, Gouda, and bacon. Add the mix to the bread machine. Make a well in the ingredients and add the yeast to it. Program the machine for Basic, select Light or Medium crust, and press Start.

When the loaf is done, remove the bucket from the machine. Let the loaf cool for 5 minutes, then turn the bucket upside-down and gently shake it to remove the loaf. Transfer to a wire rack to cool completely. Store in a sealed plastic bag at room temperature for up to 3 days, or freeze in a sealed plastic bag with the air pressed out for up to 2 months.

Cheesy Mustard Loaf

1¾ cups (420 ml) lukewarm water (100°F to 110°F, or 38°C to 43°C)

¼ cup (60 g) Dijon mustard

2 tablespoons (30 ml) canola oil

1 tablespoon (12.5 g) granulated sugar

1 teaspoon sea salt

3 cups (360 g) white bread flour

1½ cups (187.5 g) whole wheat flour

1¾ teaspoons instant dry yeast, or bread machine yeast

½ cup (62.5 g) diced (¼-inch, or 6 mm, chunks) Swiss cheese

Yield: 1 loaf

PREP TIME: 15 minutes

RISE TIME AND COOK TIME:
2-pound (908 g)/Basic program

Mustard is the condiment of choice for my family. It isn't unusual to see four or five types lined up on the refrigerator door. Regular ballpark mustard, mouth-scorching Keen's, honey mustard, grainy mustard, and, of course, Dijon. Dijon adds heat, deep flavor, and a hint of yellow coloring to the loaf, pairing well with chunks of tasty Swiss cheese. This is my go-to loaf when making Reuben sandwiches because you only have to add the corned beef and sauerkraut.

In the bucket of a bread machine, combine the water, Dijon, oil, sugar, and salt. Add the flours and yeast. Program the machine for Basic, select Light or Medium crust, and press Start.

When the machine signals, add the cheese.

When the loaf is done, remove the bucket from the machine. Let the loaf cool for 5 minutes, then turn the bucket upside-down and gently shake it to remove the loaf. Transfer to a wire rack to cool completely. Store in a sealed plastic bag at room temperature for up to 3 days, or freeze in a sealed plastic bag with the air pressed out for up to 2 months.

Garlic Mozzarella Bread

Garlic bread fans in your family will rejoice when they catch the scent of this golden, fragrant bread baking. It smells like pizza, cheese-topped garlic bread, and an Italian kitchen. For a truly scrumptious loaf, use 1 heaping tablespoon roasted garlic instead of fresh minced. You can purchase premade roasted garlic in tubes in the produce section of the supermarket or you can roast your own.

½ cup (120 ml) lukewarm milk (100°F to 110°F, or 38°C to 43°C)

½ cup (120 ml) lukewarm water (100°F to 110°F, or 38°C to 43°C)

2 tablespoons (30 ml) melted butter

1 tablespoon (20 g) honey

1 teaspoon minced garlic

1¼ teaspoons sea salt

3¼ cups (390 g) white bread flour, plus more for the work surface

2¼ teaspoons instant dry yeast, or bread machine yeast

2 cups (250 g) diced (¼-inch, or 0.6 cm, chunks) mozzarella cheese

In the bucket of a bread machine, combine the milk, water, melted butter, honey, garlic, and salt. Add the flour and yeast. Program the machine for Dough and press Start.

When the machine signals, add the cheese.

Line a baking sheet with parchment paper and set aside.

When the cycle is complete, turn the dough out onto a lightly floured work surface, punch it down, and shape the dough into 2 loaves, using your hands to tuck the bottom edges under tightly. Place the loaves on the prepared baking sheet about 6 inches (15 cm) apart, cover with a clean kitchen cloth, and set aside to double, about 1 hour.

Using a sharp knife, cut an "X" in the tops of the loaves.

Preheat the oven to 375°F (190°C).

Bake the bread until golden brown, 35 to 40 minutes. Let the bread cool completely, then store in a sealed plastic bag at room temperature for up to 3 days, or freeze in a sealed plastic bag with the air pressed out for up to 2 months.

Yield: 2 loaves

PREP TIME: 15 minutes

RISE TIME: Dough program plus 1 hour

COOK TIME: 40 minutes

Caramelized Onion Bread

1 tablespoon (14 g) butter, plus 1½ tablespoons (23 ml) melted butter, divided

1 large sweet onion, thinly sliced

⅔ cup (160 ml) lukewarm milk (100°F to 110°F, or 38°C to 43°C)

⅔ cup (160 ml) lukewarm water (100°F to 110°F, or 38°C to 43°C)

1½ tablespoons (18.75 g) sugar

1½ teaspoons sea salt

4 cups (480 g) white bread flour

2 teaspoons instant dry yeast, or bread machine yeast

Yield: 1 loaf

PREP TIME: 20 minutes

RISE TIME AND COOK TIME: 2-pound (908 g)/Basic program

Perfectly caramelized onions are a culinary revelation. How can slow cooking a pungent vegetable create mellow sweet goodness perfect for bread, soups, and many other dishes? Choose sweet onions, such as Vidalia, for this bread because the natural sugars in the allium cook to a golden brown with no added ingredients. White or Spanish onions can be used, as well, but you might want to sprinkle in a little baking soda or sugar to speed the process.

In a medium skillet over medium-high heat, melt 1 tablespoon (14 g) of butter. Add the onion and sauté until golden brown and caramelized, about 10 minutes. Set aside to cool.

In the bucket of a bread machine, combine the caramelized onion, milk, water, sugar, 1½ tablespoons (23 ml) of melted butter, and salt. Add the flour and yeast. Program the machine for Basic, select Medium crust, and press Start.

When the loaf is done, remove the bucket from the bread machine. Let the loaf cool for 5 minutes, then turn the bucket upside-down and gently shake it to remove the loaf. Transfer to a wire rack to cool completely. Store in a sealed plastic bag at room temperature for up to 3 days, or freeze in a sealed plastic bag with the air pressed out for up to 2 months.

If you do not have time to caramelize the onion perfectly, use the store-bought fried onion products in place of fresh. This will change the texture of the bread slightly and the product will break up to infuse the interior, giving the entire loaf a nice onion flavor.

Wild Rice Bread with Pumpkin Seeds

- -

1½ cups (247.5 g) cooked wild rice

1 cup (240 ml) lukewarm milk (100°F to 110°F, or 38°C to 43°C)

½ cup (160 g) honey

3 tablespoons (45 ml) melted butter

1½ teaspoons salt

3 cups (360 g) bread flour

½ cup (64 g) rye flour

½ cup (78 g) rolled oats

2¼ teaspoons instant dry yeast, or bread machine yeast

½ cup (113.5 g) pumpkin seeds (pepitas)

Yield: 1 loaf

PREP TIME: 10 minutes

RISE TIME AND COOK TIME:
2-pound (908 g)/Basic program

I live in Northern Ontario, Canada, where wild rice is indigenous. Wild rice is the seed from a semi-aquatic grass, so not rice at all. This ingredient can be a bit more expensive than other grains because cultivation and harvest are difficult, but the incredible taste and chewy texture are worth the cost. Wild rice holds its form when baked in bread, so you get a unique texture and gorgeous dark-flecked slices to enjoy with your favorite sandwich fixings. Creamy cranberry-studded chicken salad is heavenly paired with this bread.

In the bucket of a bread machine, combine the wild rice, milk, honey, melted butter, and salt. Add the flours, oats, and yeast. Program the machine the for Basic, select Light or Medium crust, and press Start.

When the machine signals, add the pumpkin seeds.

When the loaf is done, remove the bucket from the machine. Let the loaf cool for 5 minutes, then turn the bucket upside-down and gently shake it to remove the loaf. Transfer to a wire rack to cool completely. Store in a sealed plastic bag at room temperature for up to 3 days, or freeze in a sealed plastic bag with the air pressed out for up to 2 months.

Green Olive Country Loaf

1½ cups (360 ml) lukewarm water (100°F to 110°F, or 38°C to 43°C)

2 teaspoons sugar

1½ teaspoons sea salt

½ teaspoon garlic powder

½ teaspoon chopped fresh thyme leaves

3¾ cups (450 g) white bread flour, plus more for the work surface

1½ teaspoons instant dry yeast, or bread machine yeast

1 cup (100 g) chopped green olives

Canola oil, for preparing the baking dish and loaf

Yield: 1 loaf

PREP TIME: 10 minutes

RISE TIME: Dough program plus 1 hour

COOK TIME: 35 minutes

Imagine a thick-crusted loaf of piping hot bread generously studded with salty olives paired with sizzling grilled steaks or a perfectly baked fillet of fish. Look no further than this old-fashioned recipe. This loaf can be made with either black or green olives, although I find the slightly brinier green fruit tastes a bit better.

In the bucket of a bread machine, combine the water, sugar, salt, garlic powder, and thyme. Add the flour and yeast. Program the machine for Dough and press Start.

When the machine signals, add the olives.

Lightly coat a 9-inch (23 cm) baking dish with oil and set aside.

When the cycle is complete, transfer the dough to a lightly floured work surface. Pull one side of the dough up to the center of the ball and gather the opposite side into the center, folding it slightly over the first side. Gather the third side and the fourth until you have a tight package.

Turn the dough over so the gathers are on the bottom, place your cupped hands on the sides of the ball, and pull the dough under on both sides, creating a smooth ball. Transfer the loaf to the prepared baking dish. Lightly coat the top of the dough with oil and cover with plastic wrap and a clean kitchen cloth. Set aside until doubled, about 1 hour.

Preheat the oven to 400°F (200°C).

Bake the bread until golden brown and it sounds hollow when tapped (be careful; it will be hot!), 30 to 35 minutes. Let the bread cool completely, then store in a sealed plastic bag at room temperature for up to 4 days, or freeze in a sealed plastic bag with the air pressed out for up to 2 months.

Olive trees are one of the oldest cultivated tree, and humans have been harvesting the fruit for more than 8,000 years. Olives are a popular crop grown for both fruit and oil and, although some producers harvest using mechanized "tree shakers," most higher quality olives are still taken off the tree by hand. Olive trees do not grow different colors of fruit; green olives are just fruit not yet ripened to a darker color, such as light brown, purple, and black.

Mediterranean Loaf

½ cup (120 ml) lukewarm water (100°F to 110°F, or 38°C to 43°C)

½ cup (120 ml) lukewarm whole milk (100°F to 110°F, or 38°C to 43°C)

½ cup (120 g) sun-dried tomato pesto

2 tablespoons (25 g) granulated sugar

2 tablespoons (30 ml) canola oil, plus more for preparing the loaf pan

¾ teaspoon sea salt

3 cups (360 g) white bread flour, plus more for the work surface

¼ cup (25 g) grated Asiago cheese

2¼ teaspoons instant dry yeast, or bread machine yeast

Yield: 1 loaf

PREP TIME: 10 minutes

RISE TIME: Dough program plus 2 hours

COOK TIME: 32 minutes

Sun-dried tomato pesto is a food group in my house. I often catch my husband eating spoonfuls right out of the jar while standing furtively in front of the refrigerator. We toss pasta in it, top baked fish and chicken with a generous spoonful, use the pesto in salad dressing, so why not mix it into bread? The bread's interior turns a pretty shade of red or pink and the crust is a luscious golden brown when baked. You can sprinkle the Asiago on top of the bread or add it into the dough with the flour. Either choice is equally tasty.

In the bucket of a bread machine, combine the water, milk, pesto, sugar, oil, and salt. Add the flour, Asiago, and yeast. Program the machine for Dough and press Start.

When the cycle is complete, remove the dough from the bucket and gather it into a ball. Place the dough in a lightly oiled bowl, turning to coat with the oil. Cover with plastic wrap and a clean kitchen cloth and set aside until doubled, about 1 hour.

Lightly coat a 9 × 5-inch (23 × 13 cm) loaf pan with oil and set aside.

Punch down the dough and transfer it to a lightly floured work surface. Roll the dough into a 16 × 8-inch (40.5 × 20 cm) rectangle. Turn the dough so the long length stretches away from you. Staring at the closest end, tightly roll the dough jelly roll style, pinching the edges to seal. Place the dough, seam-side down, in the prepared pan. Cover with a clean kitchen towel and set aside to rise until doubled, about 1 hour.

Preheat the oven to 350°F (180°C).

If you did not add the cheese with the flour, sprinkle the dough with it now. Bake the bread until golden brown and the internal temperature reaches 200°F (93°C), 30 to 32 minutes.

Let the bread cool completely, then store in a sealed plastic bag at room temperature for up to 5 days, or freeze in a sealed plastic bag with the air pressed out for up to 2 months.

Cinnamon Swirl Bread

½ cup (120 ml) lukewarm whole milk (100°F to 110°F, or 38°C to 43°C)

½ cup (120 ml) lukewarm water (100°F to 110°F, or 38°C to 43°C)

⅓ cup (67 g) granulated sugar, divided

3 tablespoons (42 g) butter, at room temperature, divided

¾ teaspoon sea salt

3 cups (360 g) white bread flour, plus more for the work surface

2¼ teaspoons instant dry yeast, or bread machine yeast

Canola oil, for preparing the bowl and loaf pan

2 teaspoons ground cinnamon

Yield: 1 loaf

PREP TIME: 10 minutes

RISE TIME: Dough program plus 1 hour

COOK TIME: 32 minutes

Besides adding a lovely warm flavor to the bread and pretty reddish color to the swirl pattern, cinnamon can also prevent mold growth. This means the bread can stay fresh longer at room temperature.

Pinwheel bread is fun and charming. The trick to creating a perfect spiral is to roll the dough very tightly before placing it in the loaf pan. Don't worry if the layers loosen a bit when you cut off the middle slices; the bread will still taste delightful. Toast this bread and top it with butter and a sprinkle of brown sugar for perfect cinnamon toast.

In the bucket of a bread machine, combine the milk, water, 2 tablespoons (25 g) of sugar, 2 tablespoons (28 g) of butter, and salt. Add the flour and yeast. Program the machine for Dough and press Start.

When the cycle is complete, remove the dough from the bucket and gather it into a ball. Place the dough in a lightly oiled bowl, turning to coat with the oil. Cover the bowl with plastic wrap and a clean kitchen cloth and set aside until doubled, about 1 hour.

Lightly coat a 9 × 5-inch (23 × 13 cm) loaf pan with oil and set aside.

Punch down the dough and transfer it to a lightly floured work surface. Roll the dough into a 16 × 8-inch (40.5 × 20 cm) rectangle.

In a small bowl, stir together the remaining 5 tablespoons plus 1 teaspoon (42 g) of sugar and the cinnamon. Sprinkle the cinnamon mixture evenly over the surface of the dough, leaving about ½-inch (1 cm) border around. Turn the dough so the long length stretches away from you and tightly roll the dough jelly roll style from the closest end. Pinch the edges to seal.

Place the rolled dough, seam-side down, in the prepared pan. Cover with a clean kitchen towel and set aside to rise until doubled, about 1 hour.

Preheat the oven to 350°F (180°C).

Bake the bread until golden brown and the internal temperature reaches 200°F (93°C), 30 to 32 minutes. Brush with the remaining 1 tablespoon (14 g) of butter and let cool. Store in a sealed plastic bag at room temperature for up to 5 days, or freeze in a sealed plastic bag with the air pressed out for up to 2 months.

ACKNOWLEDGMENTS

I am grateful to the team at The Quarto Group for their hard work and for giving me the opportunity to create a book that has reignited my passion for bread. Thank you to all the chefs, suppliers, farmers, and home cooks over the last thirty-five years who contributed to my knowledge of food and imparted their passion for exceptional ingredients and wonderful recipes.

ABOUT THE AUTHOR

Michelle Anderson is the author or ghostwriter of more than forty cookbooks focused on delicious food and healthy diets. She worked as a professional chef for more than twenty-five years, honing her craft overseas in North Africa and all over Ontario, Canada, in fine dining restaurants. Michelle also worked as a corporate executive chef for Rational Canada for four years, collaborating with her international counterparts and consulting in kitchens all over Southern Ontario and in the United States. Michelle ran her own catering company and personal chef business, and was a wedding cake designer, as well. Her focus was simply creating delicious food and using wholesome, quality field-to-fork ingredients in vibrant, visually impactful dishes. Michelle lives in Temiskaming Shores, Ontario, Canada, with her husband, two sons, two Newfoundland dogs, and three cats.

INDEX

200